*TWAYNE'S WORLD AUTHORS SERIES*

*A Survey of the World's Literature*


# FRANCE


Maxwell A. Smith, Guerry Professor of French, Emeritus
The University of Chattanooga
Former Visiting Professor in Modern Languages
The Florida State University

**EDITOR**

*Tristan Corbière*

TWAS 511

Tristan Corbière

# TRISTAN CORBIÈRE

By ROBERT L. MITCHELL

*Ohio State University*

**TWAYNE PUBLISHERS**

A DIVISION OF G. K. HALL & CO., BOSTON

Published in 1979 by Twayne Publishers,
A Division of G. K. Hall & Co.
All Rights Reserved

Printed on permanent /durable acid-free paper and bound
in the United States of America

*First Printing*

**Library of Congress Cataloging in Publication Data**

Mitchell, Robert L    1944–
Tristan Corbière.

(Twayne's world authors series  ;  TWAS 511  : France)
Bibliography:  p. 151–57
Includes index.
1.   Corbière, Tristan, 1845–1875—Criticism and interpretation.
PQ2211.C32Z788    841′.8    78-18433
ISBN 0-8057-6352-X

For Nathan, Irma, and Stephen Mitchell

# Contents

# About the Author

Robert L. Mitchell was born on November 6, 1944, in Brooklyn, New York. He received his B.A. from Williams College, M.A. from Columbia University, and Ph.D. from Harvard University. A recipient of Woodrow Wilson and Fulbright fellowships, he has taught at the Lycée David d'Angers (Angers), Purdue University, and Harvard, and is presently Assistant Professor of Romance Languages and Literatures at The Ohio State University. Dr. Mitchell is the author of *The Poetic Voice of Charles Cros: A Centennial Study of His Songs* (University, Miss.: Romance Monographs, 1976), the editor of the forthcoming *Pre-text/Text/Context: Essays on Nineteenth-Century French Literature*, and has published numerous articles (including pieces on Corbière, Cros, Laforgue, Baudelaire, Verlaine, and Mallarmé) and reviews in European and American journals. He is presently preparing the volume on *Jules Laforgue* for the Twayne's World Authors Series.

# Preface

Most of the civilized world has no inkling of who Tristan Corbière was. What is worse, most students and scholars of French literature don't either. Fortunately, Corbière has begun to receive the critical attention he deserves, thanks to a handful of literary critics who have recently produced books about his life and his poetry (beginning with the publication of Albert Sonnenfeld's *L'Œuvre poétique de Tristan Corbière* in 1960). Yet these volumes are addressed primarily to the serious literary scholar and are all written in French. There is still no book in English on Corbière intended for readers of all levels—from the interested "general reader" to high-school and college students to teachers and professional scholars. This is the specific gap which the present volume hopes to fill.

My primary aim is to present Tristan Corbière the (forgotten) man in relationship to his (forgotten) work. Why even today so few Frenchmen and even fewer of non-Gallic descent are aware of Corbière, why such a great number of critical works and anthologies of modern poetry neglect this truly modern poet are questions which I should attempt to answer before proceeding further. There are five possible answers. Corbière was a relatively precocious writer (he never reached the age of thirty), a fact which (as for others like Rimbaud, Germain Nouveau, Laforgue, Lautréamont, and Radiguet) made his acceptance based on certain traditional critical standards (maturity, longevity) rather difficult, to say the least. He was, in one sense, a "provincial" poet (hailing from, and writing about, Brittany), lacking the qualities (sophistication, urbanity, control) of a "French" (Parisian) writer so pleasing to the sensibilities of the traditional reading audience. He was a "poet of a single volume," thus limited in regard to quantity and diversity. He was a peripheral figure, a status which frustrates the passion for categorizing (e.g., into Romantic, Parnassian, or Symbolist "schools" of poetry) which obsesses so many literary critics. Finally, he has suffered from what might be termed an "underdog syndrome." Like his contemporaries Charles Cros, Isidore Ducasse (Lautréamont), and Germain Nouveau, his refusal to submit to the rules and mores of his society has repelled readers and critics alike, who classify his life and work as "profane," thus reducing his chances for ultimate recognition. (The notable exception is Rimbaud.) The poetry of these figures has, until very recently, remained unheard of, unread, and unappreciated. At the risk of sounding sentimental, I would suggest that the critic of this type of writer must be motivated not only by aesthetic concerns, but also by compassion and a hatred of injustice. And as readers, we should not feel sorry for Corbière the man (although we do), but rather for Corbière the neglected poet.

This book is intended as a critical and analytical introduction to Corbière's verse, aimed at demonstrating, in the process, its importance in the context of French literature before, during, and after the historical period in which he lived. Because of space limitations, it is not my intention to study, or even mention, all of the some one hundred poems included in Corbière's only volume, *Les Amours jaunes*. Instead, I shall concentrate on approximately twenty texts (some of which are studied here for the first time), taken from all seven parts of the collection, which I consider to be most typical in terms of theme and poetic technique. Although discussing briefly many of the other poems in *Les Amours jaunes*, I shall depart from the traditional tendency (and departure from the norm, as we shall soon discover, is altogether fitting for Corbière) to "fragment" Corbière's poetry, that is, to cite short passages from different poems to demonstrate some stylistic or thematic idiosyncrasy, by offering detailed analyses of these principal poems presented in their entirety (or, in the case of lengthy texts, of significant passages). This feature, in addition to shedding light on the divergencies and contradictions in current Corbière scholarship, will hopefully provide insights into Corbière's thinking and writing processes for scholars and general readers alike.

The five principal chapters of this book form two groups. The first three present the essential features and paradoxes of the poet's life, the literary influences of the period in which he lived, and his method of writing poetry; the final two study the elaboration of the major themes of his poetry (isolation, love, his native Brittany, death). This organization will, I believe, permit the reader to become fully prepared for a purposely gradual exposure to the poetry itself.

All French-to-English translations are my own. Because I strongly believe that literal translations (which simply convey the *meaning* of the original) short-change the reader who does not have sufficient background in French to fully appreciate the original texts, I have attempted to "imitate" (to use an expression of Robert Lowell's) as closely as possible the poems written by Corbière, to "carry across" (trans-late) not only the general meanings, but the rhyme schemes, rhythmic patterns, linguistic idiosyncrasies and ambiguities (whenever possible), and, most important, the unique tone and texture of the language of Corbière which are so easily lost when taken out of their original French context. I hope that the non-French reader will then be able to apply the translations meaningfully to the discussions which surround them; and that Robert Frost's remark, "poetry is what is lost in translation," may be less appropriate here than usual.

I would like to express my thanks to M. François Chapon, *conservateur* of the Bibliothèque littéraire Jacques Doucet (Sainte-Geneviève) in Paris for his help in acquiring the reproduction of the frontispiece self-portrait (an etching taken from the original 1873 edition of *Les Amours jaunes*); to Professor Stirling Haig, editor of *French Review*, for permission to reprint portions of articles which originally appeared in this journal; to the College of Humanities of The Ohio State University for a Grant-in-Aid which helped subsidize the preparation of the manuscript; to Ms. Renée Kingcaid for her diligence in the typing of the final draft; and, most particularly, to Professor Laurence M. Porter of Michigan State University, whose keen critical eye was the source of numerous improvements during the final stage of preparation. Finally, I am deeply grateful to my wife, Barbara, and to my children, Noah and Jennifer, whose love and understanding—through prolonged periods during which their husband and daddy was absent, late, or preoccupied—I shall never forget.

ROBERT L. MITCHELL

*Columbus, Ohio*

# Chronology

1845    July 18: birth of Édouard-Joachim Corbière in Coat-Congar, near Morlaix (Brittany), son of Antoine-Édouard Corbière and Marie-Angélique Puyo. Spends childhood on rented estate, "Le Launay," just outside Coat-Congar.

1859    Enters *Lycée Impérial* of Saint-Brieuc. Tristan is a poor student, except in Latin and French. First attacks of rheumatism.

1860    February: writes first recorded poem, "Ode au chapeau...," about history teacher's hat. August: bad health forces Tristan to leave school in Saint-Brieuc. October: transfers to *Lycée de Nantes*.

1862    Violent attack of rheumatism, first symptoms of tuberculosis. Abandons studies.

1863    Moves to parents' summer home in Roscoff.

1864–    Composition of some of *Gens de mer*.
1868

1869–    December-March: travels to Italy with painters Jean-Louis
1870    Hamon and Jean Benner.

1871    Spring: arrival at *Le Gad Inn* of Count Rodolphe de Battine, accompanied by his mistress, the Italian actress Armida-Josefina Cuchiani (theater name: "Herminie"), baptized by the love-stricken Corbière as "Marcelle." Corbière befriends the couple, inviting them to sail on his cutter, *Le Négrier* (named after his father's best-known novel), and on his yacht, *Le Tristan*. Composition of "La Pastorale de Conlie" and "La Rapsode foraine et le pardon de Sainte-Anne." October: Rodolphe and Marcelle return to Paris.

1872    Spring: Tristan moves to Paris. Writes some of poems in *Les Amours jaunes*, *Sérénade des Sérénades*, and *Raccrocs*.

1873    August: *Les Amours jaunes* published by Glady Bros. It is a total failure, reviewed only by *La Renaissance littéraire et artistique*.

1874    *La Vie parisienne* publishes two prose works, *Casino des trépassés* (September 26) and *L'Américaine* (November 28). December 20: Corbière is found unconscious on the floor of his Paris apartment, rue Frochot. Brought to Dubois Hospital, where he remains for eighteen days.

1875   January 6: Corbière's mother brings him home to Morlaix. March 1 (10:00 P.M.): Corbière dies at age twenty-nine. September 27: Corbière's father dies at age eighty-two.

1883   Verlaine's *Les Poètes maudits* appears in *Lutèce*, to be published by Léon Vanier in April of the following year.

1891   June 17: Corbière's mother dies at age sixty-five.

## CHAPTER 1

# Introduction: Tristan WHO?

## I  Introduction to a Nonbiography

THOSE familiar with French literature and its history might ask: "*Why* Corbière? After all, he is not generally found in anthologies or bibliographies; he is not considered part of the fabric of the nineteenth-century French literary tradition; and we are, and have been, considerably more interested in 'major' poets like Hugo, Baudelaire, Rimbaud, Verlaine, and Mallarmé, as well as the various representatives of the important movements, namely, 'Romantics' (Lamartine, Vigny, Musset), 'Parnassians' (de Lisle, Banville, Hérédia, even Gautier), and 'Symbolists' (Laforgue, Régnier, Moréas, etc.)." Although it would be perhaps inappropriate, and certainly too space- and time-consuming, to argue the usefulness (or even the validity) of the latter tags here, the question as a whole is a viable one; and we shall find the answer as we turn to the life, times, and work of the poet presently and in subsequent chapters. For the time being, a more pertinent question might be posed by those less initiated to this poetic tradition: "*Who was* Tristan Corbière?" The aim of this chapter is to present the salient details of Corbière's life and to show how the important features of his development are manifested in his poetry. A study of the paradoxical nature of the poet's personality as seen in both a single poem ("Épitaphe") and *Les Amours jaunes* as a whole will then allow us to examine more specifically the relationship between theme and form, between existence and poetry, in the chapters to follow.

Unlike most writers (who, because of a robust ego and a eye toward posterity, are more than happy to furnish us with—sometimes seemingly inexhaustible—information concerning their lives), Corbière is something of a mystery. As with the life of his contemporary Isidore Ducasse, there is a distressing lack of available bio-

graphical data. What is significant, however, is that unlike the case of
Ducasse, much of the drama of Corbière's existence (that is, the
problems, anxieties, contradictions, etc., as opposed to specific
biographical facts) may be found in his verse. This is one of the many
features which make Tristan's situation in French literature a special
one, and which allow us to term the few known details of his life a
"nonbiography." Regarding his short life, there are relatively few
clues leading to *who* he was, as a glance at the spare chronology
presented at the outset of this book will confirm. Corbière's existence as a provincial recluse is in great contrast to that of his contemporaries in the limelight (e.g., Rimbaud, Baudelaire, Hugo).
His life as a "literary figure" was equally strangely anonymous and
elusive: again contrasted with French poets like Baudelaire, Mallarmé, or Valéry, he has provided us with neither critical essays on
aesthetics or the writing of poetry, nor correspondence, except for
letters written to his immediate family (the only exception—one of
sixty—is a letter to the painter Camille Dufour, written 11 July
1873); there are few clues as to how we are to date or place the
composition of his poems, since only a handful of dates appended to
poems are (possibly) authentic (the rest, as we shall see in chapter 3,
are purposely erroneous or patently ridiculous); and, because of his
isolated stature in the French literary current, he maintained no
relationships with other writers. In fact, his only "friends" were
several little-known Parisian painters, and the only writer whose
work we know he admired was . . . his father!

## II   *A Nonbiography*

Édouard-Joachim Corbière's mother was eighteen and his father
fifty-two at the time of his birth in Coat-Congar, a huge estate near
Morlaix (Brittany) left by his maternal grandfather, in 1845.[1] A poor
student who hated primary school, he read his father's novel *Le
Négrier* at the age of ten. This reading made an enormous and
immediate impression on his adolescent mind, as he followed the
adventures of sea heroes like Captain Léonard. More significant was
the permanent feeling of ambivalence toward his father produced by
these readings: an admiration of the writing itself (he later named
his cutter *Le Négrier* and dedicated *Les Amours jaunes* to his father),
undercut by a nagging resentment of the latter's popular success,

which he could never equal. This is all that we (will probably ever) know about nearly the first half of Corbière's life.

In 1859, Tristan got his first taste of estrangement: "exiled" from the family estate—the scene of what appeared to be a happy childhood—he was sent to the *Lycée Impérial* of Saint-Brieuc. His life there was miserable as a result of the pressure his parents exerted on him to do well (he was a terrible student) and of the fact that he had no friends. The situation was exacerbated by his perception of himself as hideously ugly, more so, in fact, than he actually was. Indeed, his only "model" was his father, a successful novelist, a hearty man of the sea—the exact opposite of his offspring. Corbière tried to emulate his father by writing: as a result of his oppressed condition at school (harassment by teachers, neglect by peers), his first attempts (cf. the adolescent Rimbaud) were in the parodic mode—"Ode au chapeau . . ." (leveled against his history teacher, a certain M. Lamare) and "Ode aux Déperrier," a parody of Malherbe's famous elegiac piece addressed to François du Périer—presaging the "jaundiced" verse he would later write.

Chilblain (a symptom of rheumatism) forced Corbière to leave Saint-Brieuc and travel to Nantes, where he lived with his uncle and aunt, Dr. and Mrs. Jules Chenantais,[2] and attended school as an *élève externe* (nonboarder). Even though his situation was much improved (he was part of a "home," receiving affection and no longer harassed by his teachers), Corbière's health worsened steadily: by 1862, a series of rheumatic attacks prevented him from taking his *baccalauréat* examinations. After leaving school and taking a trip with his mother to Provence, he returned to Morlaix a total invalid. Limited to sedentary activities, he began to cultivate a taste for literature, reading the "Great Romantics" (Baudelaire, Byron, Hugo, Musset, Lamartine), Villon, and, of course, Antoine-Édouard Corbière. At the same time, because of his need for love and attention, he began to play outlandish tricks and practical jokes (as elsewhere, documentation is somewhat undependable, even apocryphal), a tendency which became chronic not only in his outward behavior, but especially in his poetry, where literary "games" such as puns and parody play so large a part. It is at this time that he wrote two satires, "La Complaincte morlaisienne" and "Légende incomprise de l'apothicaire Danet," the latter written backwards with the help of a mirror!

An aggravated physical condition, in 1863, forced Corbière to move again, for the last time, to Roscoff (his parents bought a house in one of the viler sections), where he would spend most of the remainder of his miserable life. There he led a sort of maritime Bohemian existence, doing nothing much besides frequenting the inn of M. Le Gad, where fishermen and village sailors congregated. In their presence, his regret of the impossibility of participation in their activities led him to manifest peculiar, eccentric behavior. The stories—numerous and, in many cases, of dubious veracity—include his shaving his eyebrows and painting a second pair of eyes on his forehead, dressing up in outlandish sailor garb, sailing in his cutter *Le Négrier* in all kinds of stormy weather, soaking his rugs in brine, and presenting his aunt Léonie (shades of Proust!) with a bloody lamb's heart, crying, "Here, take my heart!"[3] Because of his strange appearance and demeanor, some of the superstitious Bretons called him *An Ankou* ("Specter of Death"). It is approximately during this period that Corbière assumed the pseudonym "Tristan" from his " legendary brother" (as always, the contradiction between reality and illusion is all too painful), also baptizing his scraggly spaniel with the same name. Tristan spent much of his time writing parts of the *Gens de mer* ("Sea-folk") section of *Les Amours jaunes,* drawing caricatures (at which he was rather accomplished: see the self-portrait at the front of this book), producing harsh sounds from fiddle and hurdy-gurdy (the *vielle,* a traditional Breton instrument), and befriending the Parisian artists who came to Roscoff in the summer (Camille Dufour, Charles-Émile Jacque, Gaston-Ernest Lafenestre, Michel Bouquet, Jean-Louis Hamon, et al.)[4] and who appreciated his perverse pranks. (He was said, for example, to have left his mutt on an enormously long leash, which resulted in the collective tripping of many of the unappreciative Roscovites.) Consistent with the evanescence of biographical evidence, there is a complete gap of information between 1863 and 1869.

After traveling through Italy (December 1869–spring 1870) with Jean-Louis Hamon and the Alsatian painter Jean Benner (whom the two met at Capri), Tristan returned to Morlaix, where, clad in a Pope's robe and miter (a souvenir of his visit to Rome), he made obscene gestures of benediction to the disgruntled passersby. Then, back to Roscoff, where Tristan again became painfully conscious of his physical condition, witnessing his Breton compatriots go off to fight in the Franco-Prussian War. Left alone with no audience to enjoy his farcical antics, he again sublimated his distress in flights of fantasy, which included sleeping in a small boat in the middle of his living room.

In the spring of 1871, the one major event in an otherwise non-descript existence occurred: the arrival at Le Gad's Inn of the thirty-four-year-old Count Rodolphe de Battine (who had come to convalesce from wounds inflicted near Le Mans) and his mistress, the Italian-born Parisian actress, Armida-Josefina Cuchiani. Tristan immediately swooned over "Herminie" (her stage name), dubbing her (as had been his wont) "Marcelle." The dashing count, the less-than-noble denizen of the wicked stage, and the pitiful Tristan formed, no doubt, a rather bizarre *ménage à trois*. Hardly a *ménage*, however, since it seems (again, we don't know for certain) that the relationship between Tristan and "Marcelle" was at best platonic, confirmed both in his poems and also by the fact that her devotion to the count brought them back to Paris in October 1871 . . . without Tristan. Unable to cope without this object of his infatuation, the miserable Corbière followed the couple to the capital in the spring of the following year. In November, Tristan, desperate to please the unrequiting Marcelle, dressed up as a dandy; but, like his vain attempts at maritime exploits and disguise, this ploy was a failure: thin, consumptive, and pitifully ugly, he again had but one recourse—his writing. It is during this time that Tristan wrote some of the poems in the sections entitled *Les Amours jaunes*, *Sérénade des Sérénades*, and *Raccrocs*, particularly many of the "jaundiced" love poems and "Paris" pieces which express the frustrations and scorn of his wretched existence in the French capital.

In 1873, Tristan had *Les Amours jaunes* published by Glady Bros., a disreputable firm dealing mostly in pornographic manuscripts: his father paid the subsidy. The volume (only 490 copies were printed), appearing in August, was a total failure (Corbière, typically, seemed quite unconcerned), reviewed only by Émile Blémont for *La Renaissance littéraire et artistique*, and purchased by a scant number of dirty-minded regular clients. Although Tristan kept up his writing (some poetry and two prose pieces, *Casino des trépassés* and *L'Américaine*), his health continued to decline, and on 20 December, a "friend" (once again, this anonymity is typical of the dearth of facts surrounding his biography) found him unconscious on the floor of his Paris apartment, on rue Frochot. Treated for rheumatism and pneumonia during a two-and-a-half-week stay at

Dubois Hospital, he wrote his mother, in a manner typical of the self-directed irony which marks much of his verse (playing on the word for "wood," *bois*): "Je suis à Dubois dont on fait les cercueils" ("I'm at Dubois' where they make coffins"). His mother transported him to Morlaix, where he died on 1 March 1875, at the age of twenty-nine.

### III   *The Major Threads of a "Décousu"*

The legacy of Tristan Corbière is not to be found in his life, but in his verse; although the first obviously contributed to, and represented the genesis of, the second, it would be a mistake to over-emphasize the intrinsic value of the biographical detail. There are, after all, many poets whose lives are more fascinating than Corbière's, but whose verse is far inferior. Instead, the very general preceding description of Tristan's existence—from which many minor details have been omitted—should enable us to proceed to the more essential problem of the relationship between his life and his poetry.

Corbière's nonbiography is characterized by constant contradictions, gaps, absences of documentation, hypotheses, and imprecisions. (Unmentioned were other problems: Was Marcelle a blonde or a brunette? Was Tristan afflicted with deafness? consumption? rheumatism alone? insomnia? a little of each?) In fact, if we read Tristan's "biographer," René Martineau, and his successors, we find that the sources for biographical documentation are very sparse indeed. Rather than join some of Corbière's critics in the losing battle of attempting to put the pieces of his fragmented life together, either from documents (which don't exist) or even from the poetry (which presents the same problems and erases the same traces), we should proceed in the opposite direction by seeing how this very contradiction and (apparent) confusion manifest themselves in his poetry and how the main threads of his development shaped the tone, the mood, the style—in fact, the entire orientation—of his verse.

On the basis of what we now know of Tristan's life, we might select as its five major features the following: revolt (the subject of chapter 2), the poetry itself (chapter 3), isolation or exile and heterosexual love (chapter 4), and Corbière's native Brittany (chapter 5). And it is precisely these elements which are leitmotifs throughout his poetry. The question now arises: "If Tristan's life was, admittedly, an unmitigated disaster, what, then, was the function of his poetry?" It would be natural to respond that its function was simply cathartic, that is, a form of masochistic confession, a way of venting his feelings, even a formal means of self-flagellation. But this would categorize Corbière, depending on how we look at it, as either a "Romantic" or a "Realist"; and, judging from the poetry, our instincts tell us that Tristan would shudder at such (or *any*, for that matter) categorization. Rather, we may suppose (a good rule of thumb with Corbière: *nothing is certain,* and we can take very little for granted) that his poetry is basically an act of compensation, of making up, or looking, for what was missing in his "real" existence. Tristan's poetry is, like Rimbaud's, one of self-searching (in "Décourageux," he is a "chercheur infatigable," a "tireless seeker"): the important difference is that whereas the latter wished to deform himself through new poetic language (see his celebrated letter of 15 May 1871 to Paul Demeny), Corbière, already "deformed," attempted to *define* himself. Their efforts are actually antithetical: Rimbaud's, to be visionary, Corbière's, to be lucid.

The major threads of Corbière's life can now be seen in the context of his poetry: frustration and repressed desires seek an outlet, failure seeks (potential) success, nightmares seek dreams, unrequited love seeks attention, isolation seeks solidarity, impotence and rejection seek consolation, a mute rebelliousness becomes a cry of protestation. Travel on the sea, a fantasy in real life, becomes possible in verse. Finally, and most important, "inhibition" in life becomes "exhibition" in poetry; for what Corbière the man cannot *do,* Tristan the poet can *say,* in an unrestrained manner which is his alone. The limping, dystrophic verse regales itself in triumph where the infirm, hideous body recoiled from mockery. What seems to be artifice or fantasy, even the constant preoccupation with the failures and frustrations of his doomed life, is the only reality which Corbière succeeds in mastering. Thus, the deeper motivation of his poetry is to *express* (and here we can use the word in both senses— the verbal and the "expulsive," as Francis Ponge does in his prose poem, "L'Orange") the discordance of his life and to seek a possible resolution through his writing.

The form and tone of Corbière's verse, to be discussed more fully in chapters 2 and 3, also reflect the personal qualities which characterize him. We find in his writing elements of self-pity, irony and humor, caricature, irreverence, and innovation. The desire to dazzle, the cry for attention which Corbière constantly felt, also dominate the texture of his verse. The typical Romantic cry of "épater le bourgeois" ("shock the bourgeois") becomes, with Corbière as with Baudelaire (although the former's practice is more pervasive, not limited to imagery but affecting almost every facet of his poetry), "épater le lecteur" ("shock the reader"). The innovation, the strange techniques of shock and surprise are analogues in Corbière's verse to the need to stand out, to attract attention, to assert himself, exhibited in his life. Just as the Roscovite citizenry had to become accustomed to his startling pranks, so the reader must learn to be on a constant lookout for the unexpected.

## IV   *Pose and Paradox*

Before we begin to examine the poetry itself, we should consider two features of Tristan's life/poetry which were omitted above, and which deserve special attention: pose and paradox.

The problem of Corbière's "pose," a difficult and complex one, could easily fill the pages of an entire book. Because we are concerned with other problems as well, and since many of the conclusions reached would be contradictory, we would do better to spend only a brief time on the problem in order to reach a basic understanding of its difficulties and its dynamics.

At the risk of appearing simplistic (a constant danger when we deal with the likes of Corbière), we may speak generally of two types of poses which are constantly present in Corbière's poetry. The first is characterized by role-playing, in which Corbière assumes an identity other than his own. Among his many disguises are the dog, the toad, the owl, the deaf (and blind) man, the renegade, the hunchback, the victorious (and defeated) lover, the sailor, and the pariah. As a result of his obvious human inadequacies, Corbière constantly pretended to be another whose drama he could perceive and narrate with relative impunity. The source of these personae is perhaps Corbière's adolescent reading of his father's novels, in which the adventures of sea-faring heroes (e.g., Captain Léonard of *Le Négrier*) undoubtedly gave him much vicarious pleasure. Although Corbière seems to have been as ambivalent toward his father as he was toward his own self, the fact remains that he dedicated *Les Amours jaunes* to "l'auteur du *Négrier.*" (He is said to have signed his father's personal copy with a typical wisecrack: "A l'auteur de l'au-

teur de ce livre," "To the author of this book's author.") Tristan's
initial literary pose is, of course, his pseudonym: the metamorphosis
of Édouard-Joachim to Tristan identifies the miserable wretch Corbière with his "brother," the folkloric lover, and gives to his existence a certain (mock-)heroic aura.

This brand of role-assumption is, interestingly, a perversion of
what may be termed loosely the "Romantic hero." (Romanticism,
or, for that matter, any literary "movement," was one of many
favorite targets of the keenly critical Tristan.) This figure, with variations ranging from Goethe's Werther, Senancour's Oberman, and
Chateaubriand's René to Flaubert's Emma Bovary and Stendhal's
Julien Sorel, was generally endowed with strong passions and a
healthy ego and possessed sensibilities superior to those of an unre-
sponsive milieu. In his 1805 preface to *René*, Chateaubriand described this feeling as the "vagueness of passions," where all one's
faculties, "young, active, whole, but repressed, are exercised only
on themselves, with no purpose and without a proper target." On
the contrary, Corbière has no such pride or illusions about his
"noble" character; instead, *his* isolation is an *a priori* feature of his
situation, not a result of an abortive attempt to satisfy inner passions. If Chateaubriand's description of the Romantic *état d'âme*,
the "full heart in an empty world," is "illusions good for nothing,
one is disillusioned with everything," Corbière's statement of his
own disorientation in "Épitaphe" is quite different: "Sans avoir
été,—revenu; / Se retrouvant partout perdu" ("Without having
been,—returned; / He felt himself lost at every turn"). So, beginning with a situation of isolation, and with a character not *above* the
crowd but *below* it, his tactic is a persistent metamorphosis and not
a proud assertion of his own character. Like a Romantic hero, Corbière states, in "Paria," "Je ne connais pas mon semblable" ("I don't
know my brother"). But in the next verse lies the difference: "Moi,
je suis ce que je me fais" ("As for me, I'm what I say I am"). Tristan,
a chameleon, has no true identity, no qualities resembling human,
much less superhuman, ones.

The second Corbiérian pose, more subtle than the first, is based
on self-contradiction. Our poet is constantly making statements
which contradict previous ones (as opposed to Baudelaire, for example, whose contradictions form a well-formulated dialectic), enun-
ciating sincere remarks tongue-in-cheek or gay, even sardonic ones
which apparently cover up true feelings. It is, in fact, this kind of

posing which has caused so much contradiction and disagreement among his (literary) critics. The real problem is to determine when he is sincere and when he is posing. To complicate matters, sometimes he does both simultaneously; that is, the actual pose—in the form of a contradiction, an apparently false statement or gesture, or a tautological situation—is, in reality, a statement of truth.

There is also disagreement about the motivation for this deception. Some say that the pose is a defense mechanism used by Corbière to hide his distress, to alleviate the pain of his tragic flaws by "ironic distance," a kind of counterattack aimed at those (potentially, all of us!) who don't understand him. Others, on the contrary, hold that the pose is not a mask, but a means by which Corbière attempts to find himself, to state the real truth about his (non-)identity. Since there is no real Tristan, this pose (or absence of a Tristan) *is* the real Tristan. There is surely more than a grain of truth in both of these theses, and why, indeed, should they both not be equally credible? (After all, contradictions are certainly appropriate here.) The fact remains that we should always be suspicious of what Tristan is saying, whether he means it or not: whether this deception and willed confusion is an attempt to seek or hide the truth, Corbière's poetry is marked by the elements of surprise and mischief. (We shall see this later in other curious aspects of his writing, such as chronology and "peri-text.") In a way, taking sides on this issue—often a necessary critical tool—negates the very ambiguity which informs Corbière's poetry and character alike. Perhaps there is, or should be, no satisfactory resolution of this aspect of Corbière's writing. One thing is certain, however: the reader who is not willing to be faced with this type of problem, but who is simply satisfied with the literal contents of the word as it appears on the page, should continue no further, for Corbière's poetry is meant to *trouble* and will be of little comfort in this regard.

From this discussion of the contradictory nature of Corbière's pose, it is not difficult to see how integral a part of his poetry and of his person the element of paradox is. It touches everything in his life: both the source of, and the obstacle to, his self-searching, it informs his feelings, his perception of himself, his aesthetics.

Corbière is not, of course, the only poet whose nature was paradoxical. In fact, his three most famous contemporaries—Baudelaire, Rimbaud, and Verlaine—shared this feature. But there is one essential difference which will help us put Corbière's situation in perspective: whereas the paradox of the others' lives seems to have been either chronological or localized, that of Tristan's is frenetic and pervasive. If Verlaine's life alternates between debauchery and conversion, if Rimbaud's hazardous search for a new poetic language is superseded inexplicably by the most prosaic of existences, the contradictory aspects of Corbière's life do not waver or alternate or evolve. Rather, they *are* his life. Their relationship is not one of succession, but rather of symbiosis, as one half of a contrasting pair of attitudes, statements, or drives is repeatedly sustained by its antithesis. This quality of simultaneity resembles Baudelaire's statement in *Mon Cœur mis à nu*—"There are in every man, at all times, two simultaneous postulations, one toward God, the other toward Satan"—but whereas the latter's struggle is essentially limited to a moral battle between evil and good, between *Spleen* and *Idéal*, Corbière's is not. If Baudelaire is a *homo duplex*, Corbière is a *homo multiplex*.

Since this important element of paradox will be a leitmotif throughout this entire study, only the salient characteristics need be outlined at this time. The essential point to be made is simply that the character of Tristan's life and art was such that neither could be defined or categorized. Avoid sterility, harmony, logic at all costs: this was, in short, the perception Tristan had of himself. His only uniqueness was, alas, in being such a strange nonbeing, without phylum. His poetry? Nonpoetry (at any rate, a strange, unrecognizable cacophony). Assert life? By death, sleep. Everything was undermined: the desire to succeed (e.g., as lover, sailor) by the refusal to allow himself to, even if it were possible; a need to belong, to be loved by the constant awareness of his uniqueness and isolation; the view of literature as a sincere search for identity by a hatred of directness and facility; even the pose itself by sporadic appearances of the "real" (?) Corbière (e.g., "Je suis si laid," "I'm so ugly"). The dichotomies seem endless: subjective / objective, sincerity / deception, creation / destruction, earnestness / irony, lucidity / disorientation, simplicity / complexity, Paris / Brittany, the prince / the toad. Even the title of his collection, *Les Amours jaunes* ("Jaundiced Loves")—in much the same manner as that of Baudelaire's *Les Fleurs du Mal* ("Flowers of Evil")—announces the basic paradox of the poet's situation. Rather than expand the list, let us turn to one of the opening poems of *Les Amours jaunes*, "Épitaphe," to see how Corbière states his case in his verse.

## V  *Here "lies"* . . .

At first glance, all that "Épitaphe" seems to be is a prolonged series of statements all pointing out the basically paradoxical nature of Corbière's life. But, as we should suspect by now, a "first glance" is meaningless with Corbière, since what appears to be a simple (over)statement may turn out to be something very different. Let us avoid the traditional temptation of isolating specific verses to be used as allusions to various themes which recur in other poems: the poem in its entirety has its own revelations to make concerning Tristan's art and self.

As is often the case, before we even enter the text itself (this problem of the "peri-text" will be discussed in detail in chapter 3), Corbière is mischievously dropping hints in both title and epigraph. Why is he writing his own epitaph, particularly barely after we have opened the pages of his collection? The end at the beginning? Is it all a joke, especially in the light of what follows?:

*Sauf les amoureux commençans
ou finis qui veulent commencer par
la fin il y a tant de choses qui
finissent par le commencement que
le commencement commence à finir
par être la fin la fin en sera que les
amoureux et autres finiront par
commencer à recommencer par ce
commencement qui aura fini par
n'être que la fin retournée ce qui
commencera par être égal à l'éternité qui n'a ni fin ni commencement
et finira par être aussi finalement
égal à la rotation de la terre où
l'on aura fini par ne distinguer plus
où commence la fin d'où finit le
commencement ce qui est toute fin
de tout commencement égale à tout
commencement de toute fin ce qui
est le commencement final de l'in-
fini défini par l'indéfini—Égale
une épitaphe égale une préface et
réciproquement.*

*Sagesse des nations*

(A translation would only add to the confusion! Even the most "alingual" of readers should get the message.)

Both the impossible situation of a living poet writing his own epitaph (even though it is a well-established literary tradition) and the nonsensical tautology equating beginning and end threaten to deceive us into taking the poem which follows with a grain of salt; if we are careful readers, however, we shall be able to discern the aesthetic motivation of this well-planned deception. The anachronism of the title and the paradox of the epigraph are not gratuitous, but closely tied to the poem's quintessence. Their aim and method are identical to those of the body of the poem: to arrive at the truth (or to attempt to) by telling "lies," i.e., by stating paradoxes, contradictions in terms, which themselves represent the *true* Corbière.

The title, which suggests a hypothetically premature death (ironically prescient: Tristan was to die shortly thereafter), is corroborated by statements in the poem: "S'il vit, c'est par oubli" ("If he lived, it's pure oversight"), "Il ne naquit par aucun bout" ("He was born at neither end," intimating an impossible birth), "Il mourut en s'attendant vivre / Et vécut, s'attendant mourir" ("He died expecting to live / And lived, expecting to die"). Death and life are here interchangeable, negating the positive, "living" aspect of life and ascribing to death the quality of hope and escape Corbière was not to find elsewhere. Hinted at in "Épitaphe," this theme will become more evident in subsequent poems, particularly in the *Rondels pour après*, to be discussed in chapter 5. This does, of course, echo the convoluted logic of the epigraph. The purposefully opaque rhetoric represents Corbière's ironic pose and makes fun of those who care to "philosophize"—it is signed "Sagesse des nations" ("Wisdom of nations"). But like the opening lines of Søren Kierkegaard's *The Sickness unto Death*, for example, its real intent, based on tautology, is essentially philosophical and serious. The end is the beginning, the beginning the end; Corbière's placing the life / death dichotomy in the first couplet and the final four verses surely reflects this cyclical pattern.

The poem itself is permeated with the same pose, both in regard to substance and tone. *What* Tristan seems to be saying, in a variety of ways and in almost all of the sixty verses, is that he is a "jack-of-all-trades–master-of-none." He possesses, alternately, "gold," "nerves," "verve," "soul," and "love." He is an "ideal-seeker," uses "rich rhyme," and is considered to be a "poet," "artist," and "philosopher." But every time he states a positive attribute of his own character (as he "remembers" himself) at the beginning of a verse, he immediately undercuts it (vv. 8–13):

> Du *je-ne-sais-quoi*.—Mais ne sachant où;
> De l'or,—mais avec pas le sou;
> Des nerfs,—sans nerf. Vigueur sans force;
> De l'élan,—avec une entorse;
> De l'âme,—et pas de violon;
> De l'amour,—mais pire étalon.

> *I don't know what.*—But not knowing where;
> Gold,—but not a penny to spare;
> Nerves,—without nerve. Vigor in vain;
> Verve,—with an ankle sprain;
> Soul,—and his fiddle's a dud;
> Love,—but worst stud.

In this particular stanza, we should note that the original positive statement represents Corbière's potential ("ideal") identity in the form of an abstraction, followed by a concrete entity which represents the impossibility of the potential's materializing. In each case, it is Corbière's failure in the face of the standards of society at large (no money, no verve, no attraction, no sweet music, etc.) which is in evidence. The result of these contradictions is that Tristan's very presence is eradicated, as if he never existed. Yet he did exist, and indeed, at the poem's writing, still does! What we must deduce, then, is that the only proof of his existence is in the paradox of his nonexistence. And thus we return again to the title and epigraph. *How* he seems to tell this harbors the same paradox: the tone is light and fanciful, but the aim is serious.

But "Épitaphe" is much more than a simple litany of paradoxes. If it were this alone, why carry on for sixty verses, repeating the same basic dilemma? The answer, surely, is that this is a poem, an aesthetic construct which has its own integrity, its own complexities. And here lies (the expression is appropriate!) yet another paradox, with which we shall deal in much greater detail two chapters hence: Corbière himself informs us, in vv. 19–20, that he is a "Poète, en dépit de ses vers; / Artiste sans art,—à l'envers" ("Poet, in spite of his verse; / Artless artist,—inverse"). The only way in which this can be a poem and Corbière can be a poet, we must assume, is if poetry can be written without "verses" and an artist can perform without "art." The key to the poem, and to many which will follow, is in our perception of these two vital terms. If we interpret them in their broadest sense, that is, as the accepted aesthetic norm of the period in which our poet lived, we then realize the significance of v. 29 (in fact, this may well be the single most important verse in all of Corbière's poetry)—"Ses vers faux furent ses seuls vrais" ("His false verses were his only true ones"). Corbière's intention is to write "false" (non-)verses—his only "real" ones—just as his life is "false" (a perversion of what a "real" life should be), his epitaph is false, and so on.

We can begin to see how he does this by looking at the poem's formal structure. By normal prosodic standards inherited from the seventeenth-century aesthetics of Malherbe and Boileau and maintained through the mid-nineteenth century (even though the Romantics, particularly Hugo, had begun to experiment with *enjambement*, verse length, and "accepted" poetic vocabulary), the poem is an obscenity. The only real link with "verse" or "art" is its octosyllables (the most popular verse-length in France, with the alexandrine, or twelve-syllable verse), and even this is vitiated by blasphemous inconsistency: vv. 1–3 are alexandrines, and v. 8, introducing an octosyllabic stanza, is itself decasyllabic. Otherwise, the stanzas are irregular (distich-monostich-quatrain-septet-quatrain-tercet, etc.); the punctuation proliferates unrestrainedly (e.g., three colons, twenty-two semicolons, and thirty dashes); the rhythm is noticeably abrupt and the tone is one of informality and conversation; and, finally, the syntax is elliptical, "telegraphic": after the opening seven verses, in the fifty-three remaining ones, there are only six sentences with the recognizable subject-verb sequence.

Aside from this general perversion of traditional poetic criteria, Corbière employs several devices which are ostensibly nonpoetic but which characterize his *own* brand of writing and, again, represent a sort of pose: deception, in the form of the double-entendre and the pun; and the use of verbal spontaneity to conceal an "organizing element."

On the surface, "Épitaphe" seems a pleasantly humorous piece, but Tristan is too clever a poet to let the amusement of his reader be his prime purpose. The ambiguity of many expressions in the poem reflects both his ironic stance and his desire to render the tone of his poetry strikingly personal. Indeed, he describes himself as "posant pour *l'unique*" ("posing as *unique*"). The double-entendre, a favorite practice of Corbière's, appears at the outset: "S'il vit, c'est par oubli," Tristan tells us in v. 2. The real irony of this statement lies beyond its primary (colloquial) meaning of indifference or neglect, since "par oubli," modifying the verb "to live," also suggests that the very means by which he lived was to forget his life. Furthermore, the "S'" ("Si")—"if"—which begins the verse lends an additional nuance to this ambiguity, since it is at the same time a rhetorical expression of condition ("*of course* he 's living!") and a contradiction of the premise of the poem ("but . . . he's dead!"). The "Artiste sans art,—à l'envers" of v. 20 presents some interesting possibilities. First, it may mean that Corbière is a poet who doesn't know his trade (if we interpret "art" as "aesthetics," in the sense of the contemporary "Art for Art's Sake" or as in Chénier's "Art only makes verses, the heart alone is poet"). Second, it may mean that our "poet" is "artless," without savoir-faire, playing on the two meanings for "art." Or (and Tristan should never be underestimated when it comes to word-games), if we "subtract" "art" from "Artiste" (suggested by the *literal* meaning of "sans"), we get -*iste:* it is altogether possible that here, Tristan is posing as an "-iste" ("-er"), a doer or maker or performer of any old thing (again, the "jack-of-all-trades syndrome"). The subsequent "à l'envers," then, suggests, in this case, that a "doer of any old thing" perverts the very idea of specialization which the suffix (-*iste*) connotes. In the forty-ninth verse, we read, "Ressemblant à rien moins qu'à lui" ("Resembling nothing less than himself"). This seems like a straightforward tautology, but if we pause a moment after the "rien," it may mean "Resembling nothing / (even) less than (he resembled) himself," suggesting a proximity, or at least a comparison between Tristan and . . . *zero.* Finally, in the poem's penultimate verse—"Ci-gît,—cœur sans cœur, mal planté" ("Here lies,—heartless heart, badly set")—the "mal planté" may be perceived in its ordinary, figurative sense (actually, a play on words on the fixed expression, *bien planté*); or, literally, as "badly planted," i.e., even in the ground (it *is* an epitaph, and we have just read: "Ci-gît"), Tristan's burial was botched.

The constant appearance of puns—there are thirteen in all—reflects not only Corbière's fundamental ambiguity, but also his urge to be original at any cost. (Corbière is the first poet since the fifteenth-century "Grands Rhétoriqueurs" to use the pun consistently as a poetic device.) Besides, suited to his cleverness and attitude of revolt, the pun was in appropriate contrast to the sober poetic expression of the period and in flagrant violation of its (unwritten) regulations. Several of the plays on words are based on renovations of fixed expressions. If Tristan describes himself as "Du *je-ne-sais-quoi*," he immediately undercuts this already pejorative fixed expression with one of total disorientation—"Mais ne sachant où"—by altering the form of the verb and changing its complement ("what" to "where"). The "Rime riche,—et jamais rimée" ("Rich rhyme,—and never rhymed") at first appears to be a simple contradiction in terms, impossible on the level of versification. But the irony is even more profound if we see the "jamais rimée" as an alteration of the expression *cela ne rime à rien* ("that makes no sense"): Tristan's verse is not only "unrhymed" (i.e., it *is* rhymed, but there are frequent improprieties such as identical end-rhymes, as in vv. 36–37 of this poem, or "off-rhymes"), but it also makes no "sense" whatsoever. (Ironically, this is not only ironic, but true as well!)

Our poet is equally fond of using a word in both its concrete and abstract meanings: if the tone appears "playful," let us not forget that the consequences—the ambiguous identity of Corbière himself—are most grave. Examples of this technique are, from the concrete to the abstract, "Des nerfs,—sans nerf," "Trop de noms pour avoir un nom" ("Too many names to be called something": literally, Tristan wore many "hats," including his two christened names, Édouard-Joachim, in addition to his adopted "Tristan," but in the end has no real identity, no real *nom*), "Une tête!—mais pas de tête" ("What a mug!—but nothing upstairs"), "Et fut un défaut sans défauts" ("And was an unblemished failure"); and, from the abstract to the concrete, "Brave, et souvent, par peur du plat, / Mettant ses deux pieds dans le plat" ("Brave, and often, for fear of the trite, / Putting his feet in his bite").

Accompanying these semantic gradations are a number of puns created by linguistic alteration. Tristan's thirst for the ideal is quickly undercut by his general disorientation ("Coureur d'idéal,—sans idée"); an adjective is later transformed not into a noun, but a verb, with the same self-denigrating intent—"Fini, mais ne sachant finir" ("Finished, not knowing how to end"). The adjective "fini" may mean, in addition, "having finished," or "washed up" (it *is*, after all, an epitaph), or even "finite." Another play on words is based on homophony, or identical sounds: "Prenant pour un trait le mot *très*" ("Assuming as a trait the word *quite*"). The following verse, based on antithetical adjectives ("Ses vers faux furent ses seuls vrais"), intensifies this quality of unorthodoxy which defines Corbière's personality. Elsewhere, orthographic alteration ("Prodigue comme était l'enfant / Du Testament,—sans testament," "Prodigal as the Testament's son / As for a will—well, he had none") and the addition of a prefix ("Son goût était dans le dégoût," "His taste was for the distasteful") produce similar polarities, both on the linguistic and experiential levels.

Yet another technique used by Corbière in "Épitaphe" as well as in many other poems is a type of word association, seemingly spontaneous, but nonetheless consciously designed. It is sometimes manifested in the transference of the same sound from one word to another (the opposite effect of harmony is later developed in English verse by Gerard Manley Hopkins), as in "Et musicien: de la palette. / Une tête!," or in the repitition of the same word, as in "Prenant pour un trait le mot *très* ( . . . ) Très mâle." In both cases, the initial word or sound appears at the end of a verse, the second at the beginning. More often, word "networks" are formed to organize the essential motifs. Two illustrations of this technique appear at both ends of the poem. "Son seul regret fut de n'être pas sa maîtresse" ("His only regret was not to have been his own mistress"), says Tristan, suggesting that, a total failure in regard to heterosexual relations, he alone would have been capable of satisfying (and understanding) his loneliness. Although this verse has little in common thematically with v. 7 ("Mélange adultère de tout," "Adulterous mixture of everything"), "maîtresse" does announce "adultère," thus producing a connotative link of illicitness. An intervening verse, "Il ne naquit par aucun bout," contributes the idea of reproduction, implicit in that of sexuality: in all three cases, we are witnessing phenomena which occur outside the limits of "normalcy," either relations outside the marriage bonds or a birth which is like no other (and, in fact, gynecologically impossible). The sexual motif is continued in the thirteenth verse: "De l'amour,—mais pire étalon." This time, the themes of love, sexuality, and particularly abnormality—stallions are supposed to succeed in sexual performance—are reinforced, while Corbière's nonidentity remains intact. Two verses later, he describes himself as a "Coureur d'idéal":

seemingly unrelated to the other expressions in this group, the link *can* be made—and thus the motif extended—if *coureur* is interpreted in its familiar sense of prostitution. So, the theme of illegitimacy seen in "maîtresse" and "adultère" is not only echoed here, but the very act of *striving* for the ideal is undermined by some more of Corbière's linguistic trickery. Toward the end of "Épitaphe," the "goût" ("taste") already mentioned ("Son goût était dans le dégoût") is immediately followed by two culinary expressions: "Trop cru,—parce qu'il fut trop cuit" ("Underdone,—because he was overcooked"). We cannot necessarily expect that this refers back to the stew of v. 6 ("Et fut un arlequin-ragoût," "And was a motley-stew"), but this too is not impossible. What is significant, though, is that just as the word associations previously discussed were produced, in part, by a double-entendre ("Coureur"), so here the "cuit" forms a bridge between the culinary expressions which precede and the "ivre" which follows ("L'esprit à sec et la tête ivre," "A withered mind and a drunken head"), since *cuit* can mean both "cooked" and, in the popular sense, "stoned."

The questions which these products of Corbière's poetic creativity evoke are similar to all those which surround the enigmatic creature that is Tristan Corbière. Is he really serious when he calls himself "Artiste sans art"? Is he, as he states in the final verse of "Épitaphe," "Trop réussi,—comme *raté*" ("Too successful,—as a *failure*")? Perhaps he considers himself a failure in terms of his life, but does he include his writing in the bargain? The questions are difficult, but it is clear that, after all, what Corbière leaves us as his epitaph is not an engraving or a tombstone, but a *poem*; and this very act may be seen as a contradiction to his apparent aesthetic indifference. Not only this, but he repeats the process in other poems such as "Une mort trop travaillée," "Sous un portrait de Corbière," "Laisser-courre," and "Décourageux."

As we can see from our study of "Épitaphe" and the remarks which precede it, the answer to the question in the title of the present chapter is extremely complex (if at all answerable). There are surely many poets far more difficult than Corbière, but few whose credibility and identity are so elusive. What makes his poetry so attractive is this mystery, this unpredictability, present in both the scarcity of biographical clues and the—willed—ambiguity of the work itself. To investigate his poetry further, then, we should proceed with caution, taking care not to categorize him or to make any judgment without considering the opposite alternative. In fact, the very undertaking of this book is, in a sense, hazardous in that, just as Corbière probably sensed that his ideal of knowing or defining himself, and of fulfilling this knowledge through his verse, was an impossible task, so our task of really knowing who he was is, at best, problematic. Rather than play the role of the Zen masters who often answer questions with nonanswers, one of which was simply silence (although perhaps Corbière may have approved of this method of approaching him), we might do better to take a look at the milieu in which Tristan lived, at least to put into perspective the nature of his human failures and of his special brand of poetry.

CHAPTER 2

# Corbière in Context: Malediction and Poetry in Nineteenth-Century France

## I Accursed Poets

OUTSIDE of the literary groups of the nineteenth century, isolated from the solidarity of the major "movements," and, in some instances, even exiled from the flux of human intercourse, were a number of poets who were considered *maudits*("accursed")[1] and whose individual journeys through life and literary production represent so many remarkable chapters in the history of French poetry. The poets we might consider "accursed" were, in some way, out of step with their time: outside of it (as with the "anonymous" Lautréamont), logistically (Laforgue) or spiritually (Corbière) estranged from it, or ahead of it in a visionary sense (Cros, Rimbaud, Mallarmé). A major motivation behind the *maudits'* writing was a constant experience of rejection or failure: Corbière's failure as lover and sailor; Cros's humiliation by the *Académie des Sciences*, who refused to acknowledge his scientific discoveries; Baudelaire's (and, to a lesser degree, Verlaine's) constant, losing moral struggle with the forces of Good and Evil; and Mallarmé's never-realized aesthetic obsession with creating the ultimate "Work." Even the titles of some of the *recueils* reflect internal conflict or oppression, or an ironic attitude toward the nature of things: *Les Fleurs du Mal* (Baudelaire), *Le Collier de Griffes* (Cros), *Les Amours jaunes* (Corbière), *Les Complaintes* (Laforgue).

Some of the *maudits* were also *maudisants*, converting their own feelings of being "different" from others into scorn for various elements in society. Many of Rimbaud's earlier poems were scathing attacks against the bourgeoisie, functionaries, and religion; Cros

often ridiculed the acquisitive capitalists who trampled innocent
souls like his own; Laforgue's poems frequently reflect his disdain
for bourgeois ennui and religious hypocrisy; and Verlaine, Cros,
Rimbaud (all of whom contributed to the *Album Zutique,* a collection which contained cruel and often obscene parodies of Parnassians like de Lisle, Coppée, Hérédia, and Dierx),[2] and Corbière
(particularly in "Un jeune qui s'en va" and "La Fin") all criticized
the aesthetic attitudes of more conventional poets. Furthermore,
many of these poets had the tendency of lashing out ironically at
themselves (as opposed to the Romantic melancholy plaint): examples are certain passages of Rimbaud's *Une Saison en Enfer,*
Baudelaire's "L'Héautontimorouménos," the bulk of Corbière's
poetry, Cros's "Berceuse," and Laforgue's "Complainte du fœtus de
poète."

These poets do not form a homogeneous group, but, rather, a
divergent series of isolated examples, whose struggles and poetic
visions differed greatly one from the other. The phenomenon of the
*maudit* does seem, nonetheless, curiously inherent to the literary
climate of nineteenth-century France. (We may even expand the list
to include poets like the American Poe, Nerval, and some of the
"lesser Romantics," the *bouzingots.*) With the appearance of poets
who reflected a certain solidarity with man's sentimental (Apollinaire), religious (Claudel, Péguy), or intellectual (Valéry) experience, and the return of the formal literary *cénacle* (e.g., Breton and
the Surrealists), the twentieth century has tended not to produce
such a creature as the "accursed" poet.

## II  *Corbière: A Special Case*

Even among these isolated cases, Corbière was in some ways the
most *maudit* of the *maudits.* The lives of Mallarmé, Verlaine, Laforgue, and Cros lacked the *total* isolation so characteristic of Corbière's. Mallarmé and Verlaine met with, wrote to, and conversed
with their peers throughout their literary careers (Mallarmé, we
remember, was the perpetual host of the "Tuesday evening," literary meetings); Laforgue, isolated geographically from France (he
spent five years in Germany as French reader at the court of the
Empress Augusta, from 1881 to 1886), corresponded frequently
with close friends like Gustave Kahn, Charles Ephrussi, Charles
Henry, and Léo Trézenik; and Cros, despite his disillusionment
with society at large, was active in poetic circles and, in fact, was

president of the *Zutistes* in 1883. More important, the literary development of the former three was deeply bound to poets and thinkers who preceded them: Laforgue's early verse owes a great deal to Hartmann and Schopenhauer, Verlaine's and Mallarmé's to Baudelaire and Poe. Rejection of conscious, acknowledged influence, then, in all three cases, was a gradual process; and it was this search for "models" which pervaded their early development. The same is even true for the mercurial Rimbaud, whose 24 May 1870 letter to the archconservative Banville reflects at least a temporary subservience to the "masters." And Cros's and Baudelaire's poetry remained bound to the conventional rules of prosody, even if their lives and certain aspects of their poetry (e.g., themes, imagery) were "accursed." In fact, this is Rimbaud's very criticism of Baudelaire in his famous *voyant* letter to Paul Demeny of 15 May 1871: "Still, he lived in too artistic a milieu."

In contrast, Corbière's isolation from society and particularly from his literary peers was virtually total. He corresponded and discussed with no one and, consequently, had no models for his early verse. (Indeed, the concept of "early" and "mature" poetry—e.g., the difference between Laforgue's *Le Sanglot de la Terre* and *Derniers vers*, Mallarmé's "Baudelairian" verse and his late sonnets, or Rimbaud's *Premières poésies* and his *Derniers vers* or *Illuminations*—is meaningless regarding Corbière.) Not only does Corbière's total rejection of society and of his peers isolate him from these other poets, but so does the absence in his poetry of major social themes: with the exception of "La Pastorale de Conlie" and the first stanza of "Paria," Tristan's verse is apolitical (this element appears in Cros and Rimbaud) and areligious, in the orthodox sense. (Baudelaire, Rimbaud, Verlaine, Lautréamont, and Laforgue all treat this theme to varying degrees.) What makes Corbière's drama unique in this sense is that it is entirely internalized, dispensing with the outside forces represented by his social and historical milieu. This is perhaps why, of all the *maudits*, Corbière is the only one to identify himself truly with the pariahs, the maimed, and the downtrodden of this world. (It is true that Baudelaire was also sensitive to "types" such as the old, the poor, the blind, the beggar, and especially the exiled, but his perception was far less subjective than Corbière's.)

The problem of Corbière's neglect by critics and readers exacerbates his status as a particularly isolated figure. It is true that many of the *maudits* were considered outcasts, or simply ignored, by the general public, who were more drawn to conventional verse such as that of the "Parnassian" poets, as Louis Forestier so aptly explains:

We might ponder some of the many collections which came out that year. At random, we have: *Les Poèmes dorés* by Anatole France; or: *Les Poèmes civiques* by Victor de Laprade; or still better: *Le Bleu et le noir* by André Theuriet. Chosen less at random, some better-known titles and names catch our eye. 1873 is the year in which Arthur Rimbaud's *Une saison en enfer*, (Tristan Corbière's *Les Amours jaunes*, and Charles Cros's *Le Coffret de santal* appear.
    You had to be pretty perceptive and to have had an eye for poetry to imagine, a hundred years ago, that the latter three writers would interest us, today, more than the other three. If a competition were held between them all, the die would have been cast ahead of time and some of them eliminated automatically. The victor would have been Laprade or France, maybe Theuriet; but Rimbaud, Cros or Corbière? Who knows these fellows whose names are so naturally combined to form . . . a hemistich?[3]

But the neglect of Corbière by general and critical readers had its own peculiarities. For one thing, were it not for a chance occurrence, his name might well have been consigned to the literary scrapheap. The total commercial failure of *Les Amours jaunes* (published in 1873) was shortly followed by the bankruptcy of his dubious publishers, Glady Bros. Then, in 1882, Corbière's first cousin, Pol Kalig (the pseudonym of Jules Chenantais), happened to show the poems to the editor of *Lutèce*, Léo Trézenik (pseudonym of Léon Épinette: *trézenik* means "little thorn" [*épinette*] in Breton), who in turn showed them to Verlaine. The latter was so impressed that he included Corbière in his *Les Poètes maudits*, along with the better-known Rimbaud and Mallarmé.
    Not even the notoriety of this essay, however, did much to guarantee Corbière's niche in the pantheon of French poets. Neither did Huysmans's *A Rebours*, which appeared in 1884. Perhaps this was because these writers were, in a sense, *maudits* themselves. Despite these isolated examples of "free publicity," Corbière's malediction is in part very much posthumous. (This is not surprising in the light of his ironic treatment of the paradoxical life / death dichotomy.) Critical treatment of our poet has, since his death, been negative, contradictory, or nonexistent; and, con-

sequently, his readers have been mal- or uninformed. Forestier's remark cited above does express the general prejudice against the *poètes maudits* during the time at which they wrote, but what is really quite extraordinary is that even today, more than a century later, poets like Corbière, Cros, and Germain Nouveau are just beginning to be appreciated by the reading public.

To put it bluntly—the metaphor, although a bit unsightly, is nonetheless appropriate because of its social connotation—Corbière, like a number of his contemporaries, was a blemish on the face of traditional French poetry. We can even say that (in view of his background of "estrangement") to "France, mère des arts" (Du Bellay's "France, mother of the arts"), Tristan was a *fils naturel* ("bastard son"). Early on, conservative critics were expressing their vehement disapproval of the *maudits*. In his review of Verlaine's *Les Poètes maudits*, Léon Bloy calls Rimbaud and Mallarmé "immobile poets, and solidly fixed in the same pagoda of perfect imbecility [as Corbière] where the exasperated reader can always let fly at them with dead aim his own malediction." As for Corbière, Bloy declares: "OK, but I am bewildered at the presence of Tristan Corbière in his trilogy. No one was ever more ardent and more ravaged by a more mobile lunacy than this alienated poet who flowed all over the place." In 1891, Émile Deschamps, director of *La Plume*, calls Corbière "a likable third-rate writer." Even those critics who did recognize a certain poetic talent tended to minimize Corbière's originality by comparing him either to Villon or to his father: "The preface to this novel [*Le Négrier*] reveals a mind which is rather haughty and quite disdainful of the public: the same mind with talent and a more acute irritability,—you have Tristan Corbière,"[4] or: "If we were to combine the Bohemian mind of Gérard de Nerval, the love of irony of Villiers de l'Isle-Adam, the realism and the literary optic of Villon, and the good-humored tone dear to Béranger, we would have a picture of the literary personality of Corbière."[5] Despite a relative proliferation of recent Corbière criticism, Tristan is still *méconnu*, undiscovered: only nineteen books have been written about him (median year of publication: 1948!), and in English, at last count, only three unpublished theses and a handful of articles. Taking all this evidence into account, is it any wonder that of all the original volumes on the *maudits* in the Seghers "Poètes d'aujourd'hui" series, the cover of Corbière's is the only one in black?

### III   *A Square Peg in a Round Hole*

Corbière's poetry presents an insuperable problem for those literary historians who cling to the notion that writing must be categorized, for the sake of convenience or sanity, according to "period" and "movement." Tristan's soul was fundamentally "Romantic," his interest in the autonomy of sound and its evocative capabilities was compatible with "Symbolist" doctrine, and some have likened his images to those of the "Surrealists." Although all these assertions contain a germ of truth, they are totally misleading and, in fact, conceal the real nature of Corbière's concept and practice of poetry. His verse is so striking because his attempt at expressing his true self was based on avoiding models, breaking rules, and disregarding the "code" of a prosodic system which he considered falsifying and artificial. Thus, if he seems, on the surface, to be a poet of supreme deception and posing, he is, on a more profound—motivational—level, one of unimpeachable honesty. In order to appreciate how his poetry is a radical departure from the literary context in which he wrote, we should briefly consider the type of verse written in France just before and during his tenure.

Innovations and transgressions made by "Romantic" poets may seem tame to today's reader, but at the time they were considered to be shocking. The revolt against conventional form consisted largely in the alteration or manipulation, rather than the discarding, of certain of its practices. In order that the rhythm of their verse might reflect their inner emotions, some Romantics took liberties with traditional French versification by shifting the median caesura of the alexandrine (the major pause after the sixth syllable of a twelve-syllable verse); by introducing a consistent use of *enjambement*, or the running over from one verse to the next, as in the "indecent" opening verses of Hugo's 1830 drama, *Hernani*; and by recognizing the validity of a much broader spectrum of viable poetic subjects (see Hugo's preface to *Les Orientales*) and vocabulary (again, Hugo: "I placed a cocked hat on the old dictionary"), disregarding the guidelines which were the legacy of the earlier "neoclassical" writers. The approval of this relaxation of classical rules is reflected very early in an 1819 review of André Chénier's poetry, in which an adolescent Hugo speaks of this stylistic casualness: "each of the poet's mistakes is perhaps the germ of a perfection for poetry." Despite these limited excursions into the then-uncharted waters of poetic insurrection, most of the poets of the first half of the nineteenth century still adhered to many of the basic tenets of tradi-tional French verse, including the alternation of masculine and feminine rhymes and a vague, abstract vocabulary. Furthermore, an essential aspect of much Romantic verse is the retention of the declamatory, rhetorical tone present in the French poetry of the two preceding centuries. (The prevalent conventional techniques of apostrophe, hyperbole, periphrasis, and inversion helped create this tone.) Because it went much farther than the "Romantics" in dislocating traditional French prosody and rejected an even greater number of guidelines, "cosmetic" or otherwise, Corbière's style has little in common with that of his predecessors.

But it is not only this divergence in style that estranges Corbière's poetry from the Romantics': he was equally repelled by the (in his view) pretentious overseriousness of the philosophical vein in Romantic poetry (e.g., in the verse of Lamartine, Hugo, and Vigny). Many of these poems were in the form of "meditations" or "contem-plations." (These were, in fact, the very titles of two celebrated *recueils*.) This protest is filed in "Décourageux" (a neologism mean-ing "Discouraged One"), in which Tristan characterizes himself (or his persona, which almost always represents Tristan himself) in the following manner:

> Mineur de la pensée: il touchait son front blême,
> Pour gratter un bouton ou gratter un problème
>           Qui travaillait là—Faire rien.—
>
> Thought's miner: he touched his pale forehead,
> To scratch a pimple or to scratch a hard
>           Problem which was working there—Doing nothing.—

As usual, Corbière's manner of reflection ("gratter un problème") is negated by its equivalence with the physical (dermatological) act of scratching at its most primitive level—to relieve a bothersome itch. The final verse of this passage also undercuts the motif of cerebra-tion: the "problem" which was percolating in the poet's mind is, in the end, unproductive, as the active verb "travaillait" is soon un-dermined by its opposite, "Faire rien."

If the Romantic mold was not made for Corbière, neither was the Parnassian one. Very briefly (the contrasts are not nearly as complex as those involving the Romantic poets), it was particularly the method of creation of these poets that Tristan could not accept: how different from their finely chiseled sonnets, marked by the minutest of physical descriptions, colors and textures, exotic vocabulary, and strict adherence to rules, are Tristan's ironic concoctions marked by word-play, verbal acrobatics, and blatant transgressions of all the poetic regulations! Even Banville, himself fond of verbal and rhythmic acrobatics, authored the *Petit traité de poésie française*, which, presenting all the mechanical rules of the verse, of rhyme, of hiatus and *enjambement*, of meter, and of fixed forms, could not possibly represent a poetic ideal farther from the radical one of Corbière. We shall examine Tristan's aversion to the Parnassian ideal of "plastic" art in much greater detail during the discussion of "I Sonnet" in the chapter to follow.

## IV   *That?*

Now that we know where Corbière's poetry *doesn't* fit, let us attempt to discover where it . . . *doesn't* fit! Contradictory as this assertion may sound, it is, nonetheless and typically, the way in which Tristan himself might have stated the problem. In fact, in "Ça?," the opening poem of *Les Amours jaunes*, he attempts to do just this; and this attempt to categorize his verse, to classify it (or to "unclassify" it), just as Tristan's other attempts—at lucidity, fulfillment, communication, etc.—fails miserably, or so it seems.

Even before the poem begins, we are made aware (if our attention does not wane while we turn the page) of the ironic tone that will permeate the text itself: the curious title is preceded by the title of the first section of the entire collection (which happens to be identical, except for the absence of punctuation), so that, in effect, Corbière presents us with the following imaginary dialogue:

> —Ça
> —Ça?
> —That
> —That?

The question mark after the poem's title is thus reinforced and given the power of a "double interrogative." The status of the "that" is even more suspect when we notice that it is followed immediately by another interrogative, "What? . . . ," which adds a triple-barreled dose of ridicule: it piles on another question which raises the relevance and validity of the title itself ("Ça / Ça?" / "What? . . ."). Its English phrasing implies a total lack of communication between the two parties of the dialogue (perhaps Corbière and Corbière), and, as an epigraph to the poem, its original author was none other than Shakespeare, the paradigm for eloquence in English. (There is no need to emphasize that "What?" is not one of the Bard's most eloquent pronouncements. . . .) Once we discover that "Ça" (a term which was later to become the French label for the Freudian "id") refers to Corbière's poetry, we can begin to appreciate the *apparent* denigration of the verse by its author.

The first half of the poem will give us a good idea of what Tristan is up to:

> Des essais?—Allons donc, je n'ai pas essayé!
> Étude?—Fainéant je n'ai jamais pillé.
> Volume?—Trop broché pour être relié . . .
> De la copie?—Hélas non, ce n'est pas payé!
> Un poëme?—Merci, mais j'ai lavé ma lyre.
> Un livre?—. . . Un livre, encor, est une chose à lire! . . .
> Des papiers?—Non, non, Dieu merci, c'est cousu!
> Album?—Ce n'est pas blanc, et c'est trop décousu.
> Bouts-rimés?—Par quel bout? . . . Et ce n'est pas joli!
> Un ouvrage?—Ce n'est poli ni repoli.
> Chansons?—Je voudrais bien, ô ma petite Muse! . . .
> Passe-temps?—Vous croyez, alors, que ça m'amuse?
> —Vers? . . . vous avez flué des vers . . .—Non, c'est heurté.
> —Ah, vous avez couru l'Originalité? . . .
> —Non . . . c'est une drôlesse assez drôle,—*de rue*—
> Qui court encor, sitôt qu'elle se sent courue.
>
> Essays?—Come on, I haven't tried!
> A study?—Too lazy to be a crook.
> A volume?—Too cheap to be a bound book . . .
> Copy?—No, alas, it's not subsidized!
> A poem?—Thanks, but I've hocked my lyre.
> A book?—That's still something to read, Sire! . . .
> Papers?—No, thank God, those are sewn!
> An album?—It's not blank, and too wind-blown.
> End-rhymes?—Which end? . . . And it has no grace!
> A work?—It's not polished all over the place.
> Songs?—I'd love to, my little Muse! . . .
> Pastime?—So you think it keeps me amused?
> —Verses? . . . Something flowing . . .—No, it's jerky.
> —Ah, you've run after Originality? . . .
> —No . . . *from the streets*—she's a strange hussy,
> Who scats, when propositions should keep her busy.

As we shall see so often, the contradictory relationship between content and form (*what* Corbière says and *how* he says it) is of critical importance to the full understanding of the poem. It is noteworthy that although this is one of the salient features of many of Corbière's poems (in addition to "Épitaphe" and "Ça?"), it has not, to date, received much attention.

The substance of this passage (and, for that matter, of the entire poem) may be reduced to a single (tongue-in-cheek) question posed by Tristan: "How can one categorize my poetry?" As in "Épitaphe," the propositions set forth in the first part of almost every verse (possible solutions to the central dilemma) are constantly undercut in the second. One after another, the questions become rhetorical, as the reader realizes that the poetry in question is unrecognizable, a mongrel breed. In fact, it is not poetry at all, but. . . . According to the literal meanings of the "responses" of the first four stanzas, Corbière's verse is devoid of effort, has no roots in tradition, is carelessly edited, unsubsidized, unlyrical, unreadable, unattached, incoherent, inchoate, unpolished, unmusical, unamusing, unoriginal. What is absolutely essential here is that if the poem (so far) is taken *at face value,* it would seem to be merely an exercise in frustration, even masochism. Except for one important and paradoxical fact—Corbière *is* writing a poem, and the way in which it is written is the implicit solution to the problem. Corbière's poetry may appear bizarre, but it is still poetry, in an unconventional sense. Tristan's action (the writing of the poem), in this sense, speaks more softly, and far more eloquently, than his assertions (that his verse is nonverse); and what we must now do is to examine the new "category" of poem which the actual form of "Ça?" has created.

A first glance at the poem confirms Corbière's constant claim that this does not resemble poetry, in the accepted sense (i.e., that it does not correspond to recognizable categories such as "essay," "study," "volume," "book," "work," etc.). Practically devoid of all traditional rhetorical language, "Ça?" is to be neither sung nor read (as Corbière explicitly states), but *to be said;* and it is on precisely this antirhetorical, antipoetic language and manner of expression that Corbière's new poetics is largely predicated.

The proximity between the language of the poem and "ordinary prose" (cf. Molière's M. Jourdain) is manifested to some degree in the use of colloquial or familiar locutions throughout: "Allons donc," "Hélas non," "encor," "Dieu merci," "Et," "Je voudrais bien," "alors,"

"Ah"; and, in the second half of the poem, "Eh," "Mais non," "Bon," and "Mais" (twice). The poem's physical appearance also resists rhetoric or evocative power by presenting a dialogue based on brusque questions (which cut off the usually symmetrical flow of the alexandrine—6/6 or 4/4/4—after syllables 1, 2, 3, or 4) posed by a hypothetical interlocutor. Also in contrast to the conventional lyrical elements of delicacy and evocation is the Corbiérian technique of *accumulation* (more typical in prose: a good example is the general style of Rabelais). Many "lyrical" texts are based on some kind of evolution or development from beginning to end, either linear or cyclical, which unifies the separate stanzas and allies them to a central theme or feeling or vision. With Corbière, there is no such occurrence, but rather a repetition of the same basic idea. Corbière is, in this respect, a sort of exhibitionist, showing the reader his verbal agility, his spontaneity of expression, pounding away at some obsession or another in an effort to conquer it in his own raucous way. It is—ostensibly—poetry by insistence, not insight, by persistence, not perception.

Corbière also tampers with conventional patterns of versification. If we remember that, very basically, the classical alexandrine has a caesura (major pause) after the sixth syllable (and generally two *coupes*, or minor pauses, after syllables 3 and 9) and counts twelve syllables, including unaccented final *e*'s not followed by vowels, we can see the deviations rather clearly. Pauses are not only inconsistently placed at various unexpected positions in the verse, but the syllable-count is equally unpredictable. Examples of this transgression occur in Corbière's handling of the mute *e* and of dieresis. If the mute *e* is counted in both vv. 2 ("Étude") and 4 ("copie"), the former verse contains twelve syllables and the latter thirteen. This is even more baffling if we look at v. 16, in which Corbière follows traditional poetic practice by omitting the final *e* in *encore* in order to preserve the twelve-syllable count. However, Corbière uses dieresis (in this case, the pronunciational division of the *ie* sound) and syneresis (the sliding-together of the same sound to make one syllable) as he sees fit: the former appears in vv. 7 ("papiers" counts three syllables) and 26 ("rien" counts two), the latter in v. 20 (three for "correction").

If inconsistency and surprise are anticlassical elements, so is excess, seen not only in the technique of accumulation, but also in the poem's punctuation. In order to give life to his false dialogue and to express his thoughts "out loud" rather than pronounce them in the familiar lyrical whisper, Tristan punctuates "Ça?" with thirty-four dashes, thirty-one question marks, twenty-seven commas, fifteen ellipses, ten exclamation points, a colon, and a semicolon. Also in contrast to classical "harmony" are the poem's sound patterns, frequently based on homonymy ("lyre/lire," vv. 5–6; "Mais non!/— Bon," vv. 20–21; "fait/Mais," vv. 27–28, for instance).

Corbière's irreverence in regard to classical poetic language is particularly apparent in his use of a favorite technique, the pun. The bases for word-play are varied. In two cases, variations on a similar root or verb form produce the pun: "essais/essayé," v. 1 (the literary genre is etymologically derived from the verb which follows), and "couru/court/courue," vv. 14, 16 (the two meanings of "to run" and "to proposition"). Elsewhere, the bases are synonymy ("broché/ relié," v. 3: the play is on the two meanings of *broché*— "paper-bound," close in meaning to *relié*, and "edited carelessly"), antithesis ("cousu/décousu," vv. 7–8: the meaning of the latter is either the opposite of *cousu*, "unsewn," or "incoherent"), and the figurative/literal dichotomy ("—Chose à mettre à la porte?— . . . Ou dans une maison / De tolérance.— Ou de correction?," vv. 19–20, where the *porte* of "mettre à la porte"—meaning, figuratively, "to discard"—is soon followed by the two "houses" [after proposing the ashcan for his poetry, should Tristan commit it to a brothel? a reformatory?] which refer back playfully to the literal meaning of *porte*, "door"). Depending on interpretation of meaning, *bout* may imply "conclusion," as in "Bouts-rimés" (i.e., verses based on preestablished end-rhymes), or "(either)end" (*quel bout?*). Finally, in v. 30, Tristan states, "Et mon enfant n'a pas même un titre menteur" ("And my child has no title, not even a false one"): the truth is all too real (the poem's title perfectly characterizes Corbière's poetry), but, since "enfant" is being used metaphorically (for "poem"), "titre" may also mean, besides a poem title, a child's "title," or surname.

"Ça?" is a capital document because it is such a good example of Corbière's supreme pose: the poet writing a poem about not being a poet. The pose is further perpetrated by the ambiguity of the three explicitly poetic terms—*lyre*, *Muse*, and *Art* (the poem's final verse: "L'Art ne me connaît pas. Je ne connais pas l'Art," "Art doesn't know me, and vice versa"). The three expressions represent Tristan's isolation from his fellow poets: his "lyre" is off-key, not the seven-stringed instrument of poetic tradition; his "petite Muse" bears no resemblance to Euterpe, the classical Muse of poetry who provided so much "inspiration" to his peers; and "Art," for Corbière, connotes the classical aesthetic code and has little to do with his apparent disdain for poetic creation. The revolt is aimed against Recognized Poetic Practice, the following of existing rules and etiquette. True, he does not "know" Art in this sense, but he *does* know *an art*, his own, the premises of which cannot be categorized according to traditional literary means, one which consists of those unacceptable techniques described above. Throughout his poetry, Corbière will be crying wolf, having us believe he is no poet. These cries are both true and false, and there lies the deception which is at the heart of his conception of poetry. We cannot take him at his word, yet when he refers to his book as a "honteux monstre de livre" ("a shameful monster of a book") in "La Cigale et le Poète" or to his Muse as a "Muse à la voix de rogomme" ("Muse with a beery voice") in the preface to *Gens de mer*, it is his fellow poets who fall into the trap of agreeing with him. Corbière was truly a misfit in his time, and even those who begrudged him a grain of talent were inclined to see him as a kind of *idiot savant*. *Idiot sachant* ("*knowing* idiot") is a more appropriate term, for Tristan's aptitude for poetry was no fluke, but a conscious, lucid possession, perhaps his only one in life. It is Corbière who gets the last laugh when he asks in v. 12 of "Ça?": "Passe-temps?—Vous croyez, alors, que ça m'amuse?" Amusement is hardly a viable justification for Art, but the answer to the question is "Yes!," even if the reply Corbière seems to be peremptorily evoking (both from his imaginary interlocutor and his reader) is just the contrary.

## V  *Revolting Tristan: Corbière's (Per-)verse*

Before examining in greater detail this aesthetic pose (chapter 3), we should first take a more general look at the types of techniques which Corbière uses in his poetry and which set him apart from his contemporaries.

Innovation was seen as a truly positive element by certain Romantic poets, and the novelty of Hugo's and of Baudelaire's imagery is acknowledged by some as the first breakthrough to what is considered "modern" poetry. But in neither case did the revolt involve a radical move away from classical prosody. For all their innovation, these poets still maintained certain traditional features in their verse: euphony, balance, rhetoric, and clarity (i.e., an absence of willed obfuscation). By contrast, Corbière substituted his own usage of cacophony, hesitation, orality, and lexical perversity, the combination of which was surely regarded by most as heretical and as so much gibberish. The equations which motivated Tristan's opposition to convention are actually rather simple: poetry which followed rules imposed from without was a lie, a betrayal of the true expression of the poet's inner thoughts; and verse which was unfettered by convention was free to explore the truth, unhindered by compromise. To be true to himself—a rather hazardous task—Corbière had to seek his own language, not that of others (an imperative held to by most serious poets, but in this case, the will to be totally independent was extraordinarily potent). It is one of the great ironies of literary history that much of the credit for the dislocation of the alexandrine is accorded to Verlaine, whose well-known catch-phrase "Take eloquence and wring its neck" appeared in his "Art poétique" of 1873. By then, *Les Amours jaunes,* to the knowledge of almost no one, had already been completed.

If we had to choose a single word to describe Corbière's poetry, it might be *immediacy* (yet another link between his and "modern" verse). The techniques to be described here are not important simply because they are innovative in a gratuitous sense, without purpose. Rather, they aim at a very personal type of self-expression, spontaneous and total. (The paradox of apparent spontaneity produced by calculated techniques will be examined in detail during the course of the next chapter.)

What could be more personal than setting down one's feelings and thoughts in one's *own* language, without a "middle man," without worrying about filling up the verses (although he does basically stick to the "classical" line, he is not a stickler for exact count) or exact rhyming or using "improper" vocabulary or pausing at the appropriate place or structuring one's thought for the purpose of clarity? The *cheville* ("padding"), a way of filling up the verse for correct syllable count, was not even a preoccupation of Tristan's (although it was for many of his predecessors and contemporaries).

If we were to place side by side a poem by Corbière and one by almost any nineteenth-century poet writing before him (with the possible exception of Rimbaud), the immediate and obvious differences would be two-fold. First, whereas the latter text would be limited in terms of the choice of vocabulary and "proper" phrasing,

Corbière's would contain any and every word, locution, or construction appropriate to the thought or feeling conveyed: *bien dire* ("say well') vs. *tout dire* ("say all"). An eloquent reference to this disparity appears in Corbière's own "Décourageux":

> —Chercheur infatigable: Ici-bas où l'on rame,
> Il regardait ramer, du haut de sa grande âme,
> Fatigué de pitié pour ceux qui ramaient bien . . .

> —Tireless seeker: Down here where they row,
> He watched the rowing, from atop his great soul,
> Tired from pity for those who rowed well . . .

In this sense alone, Corbière's poetry is closer to the novels of Céline or Henry Miller: it is literature of proliferation, of accumulation, a vomiting (or, in Miller's case, an ejaculation) of words, words of all kinds, taken from every nook and cranny of usage. The "mélange adultère de tout" of "Épitaphe," an ostensibly derogatory description, is also a lucid characterization of Corbière's poetry. It is a bastard breed, a mutt among the pedigree products of his peers. His verse is a seemingly endless outpouring of appositions, puns, antitheses, neologisms, clichés, colloquialisms, italicized words, slang, archaisms, technicisms, abbreviations, and borrowings.[6] This eclectic style was perfect for Corbière, since he saw himself as a mutt, raceless, homeless, collarless (whether this explains the fact that his only "friend" was his own mutt is a problem which should interest dog breeders and psychologists more than literary critics), as vv. 7–8 of "Sonnet à Sir Bob" suggest:

> Mais moi je ne suis pas *pur sang*.—Par maladresse,
> On m'a fait braque aussi . . . mâtiné de chrétien.

> But *I'm* not a *pedigree*.—By mistake,
> They made me point (er/less) also . . . a devout crossbreed.

Detailed descriptions of the various techniques of this instinctive, uninhibited style will appear in the following chapter; for the moment, let us take a look at a few of them, as a general introduction to this aspect of Corbière's verse.

It was perhaps inevitable that an "outcast" was the first to deviate seriously from most of the prescriptions of conventional verse; for one interested in maintaining socioliterary ties to have done so would have meant instant excommunication. But Corbière was not motivated solely by antisocial provocation, for his poetry is intensely personal as well. The problem for him was simply this: "How can one express the discordances and hesitations of reality with euphonious, balanced, controlled language? " It was, of course, impossible (for him, at least): he was forced to select a manner of writing which would be appropriate to what he had to express.

One of the principal techniques used by Corbière to render his verse spontaneous is aberrant punctuation. Like his unorthodox vocabulary, this technique reflects the unpredictability of his poetry. At times, there is virtually no punctuation at all (in a *juvenilium,* "Ode au chapeau," except for two commas, a parenthesis, and a period; and in "Cris d'aveugle," except for three commas), even before Mallarmé and Apollinaire. The majority of his poems, however, are overflowing with exclamation points, question marks, dashes, and ellipses (which often take up entire verses!). The rhythm which results is hesitant, limping, chaotic. A blatant example of this procedure appears in "Bonne fortune et fortune," an "antilove" poem the title of which suggests Corbière's usual misfortune in love, as in everything else. The first quatrain is entirely classical, complete with *rimes croisées* (ABAB), caesuras where they should be (6/6), and—surprise!—a fourth verse which is as symmetrical as any written by Racine:

> Moi, je fais le trottoir, quand la nature est belle,
> Pour la passante qui, d'un petit air vainqueur,
> Voudra bien crocheter, du bout de son ombrelle,
> Un clin de ma prunelle ou la peau de mon cœur . . .

> I go walking, when the weather's nice,
> Looking for the girl who, playing the triumphant part,
> With the tip of her parasol would like to entice
> A wink from my eye or the skin from my heart . . .

But when the drama begins (announced by the ellipsis in v. 4), that is, the confrontation between the female "ill-reputed" passerby and Tristan's internal hesitations, the proliferation of dashes, exclamation points, and ellipses destroys what was originally a calm atmosphere and leads the reader to a typically ironic ending, in which the lady in question gives Tristan a charitable donation (instead of the other way around), rather than the anticipated physical contact:

> Et je me crois content—pas trop!—mais il faut vivre:
> Pour promener un peu sa faim, le gueux s'enivre . . .
>
> Un beau jour—quel métier!—je faisais, comme ça,
> Ma croisière.—Métier! . . .—Enfin, Elle passa
> —Elle qui?—La Passante! Elle, avec son ombrelle!
> Vrai valet de bourreau, je la frôlai . . .—mais Elle
>
> Me regarda tout bas, souriant en dessous,
> Et . . . me tendit sa main, et . . .
>             m'a donné deux sous.

> And I think I'm content—not too much!—just to live longer:
> The beggar gets drunk, to lead on his hunger . . .
>
> One fine day—what a life!—I was doing my thing.
> —What a life, I say! . . .—At last, she came walking
> By—Which She?—The Passerby! She, with her parasol!
> Hangman's valet, I brushed her . . .—but that Doll
>
> Looked down at me, thinking it was funny,
> And . . . held out her hand, and . . .
>             gave me two pennies.

In addition to the punctuation, the constant interruption ("—pas trop!," "—quel métier!," "—Métier!," "—Elle qui?") and the repetition and qualification of terms already enunciated ("métier," "Elle") create a tone which is eminently conversational and, in effect, nonliterary. This tone—established in many other poems by the use of various techniques such as apocope (the omission of final letters or syllables: for example, throughout "La Balancelle" and in the approximation of the rugged speech of sailors in the "maritime" sections of *Les Amours jaunes, Gens de mer* and *Armor*), rhetorical questions, and unannounced thoughts (interjections, exclamations)—typifies the oral aspect of Corbière's verse, which reflects the everyday language of "people" more faithfully than the rarefied elocution of "poets." (This is one of the major influences Corbière had on T. S. Eliot, as Francis F. Burch points out.)[7]

In order to make his poetry seem spontaneous and "authentic," Corbière also takes liberties with accepted French spelling and grammar; as a result, many of his poems seem offhanded, even negligent, and thus consistent with the spontaneity with which he confronts his poetic material. In regard to the spelling, there is, as always, a critical controversy. Some contend that these errors are oversights and can be attributed to Corbière's "cultural deficiencies." P.-O. Walzer, an eminent critic of this period of French literature, says that Corbière "does not have a sense of spelling, which a glance at his early letters will show"; and Rémy de Gourmont, in his *Le Livre des Masques*, considers him "laboriously clumsy." Others, like Michel Dansel, consider this trait a conscious technique, a "will to provoke." I would agree with the latter judgment, adding that it is further evidence of the "natural" style which Corbière continually develops. Among the many spelling errors are "fidelle" ("Après la pluie"), "crû" ("Bohème de chic"), "bien sur" ("Lettre du Mexique"), and "à pieds" ("Hidalgo").[8] Grammatical errors are even more numerous and include the use of *des* (instead of *de*) with the partitive construction involving prenominal adjectives, ellipses (e.g., the omission of *ne* in negative constructions), the absence of masculine-feminine agreement of nouns and adjectives, and incorrect plural forms.

Other techniques are employed to create an element of unpredictability or movement (from one feeling or idea to the next). We have already discussed the corrosion of classical versification, but we also find an irregularity of stanzaic forms which defies the "system." Many poems, particularly lengthier ones like "Litanie du sommeil," "Le Poète contumace," and "Épitaphe," manifest a constant and unpredictable variety of stanzas which fall gratuitously on the page, seemingly as the mood strikes their creator. Even more representative of this freedom of movement is Corbière's poetic concept of word alliance or association, which is perhaps his chief contribution to "modernity" in subsequent poetry. The two principal types of association are those involving sounds and words. Poets interested in evoking a mood generally use rich rhymes and assonance to create a harmonious or "musical" atmosphere. Corbière, on the other hand, gives the impression not of controlling similar sound patterns, but of allowing himself to be transported from one thought to another at the very moment at which a particular sound is uttered. This occurs, for example, at the beginning of "Sonnet à Sir Bob," in which the two sounds [wa] and [ɛs] bring to mind other words which then dominate the stanza, at all positions of every verse (v*ois*--m*oi*-pourqu*oi*?- m*oi*-v*ois;* car*ess*er-maîtr*esse*- car*esse*-maîtr*esse).* The study of "Litanie du sommeil" will presently corroborate the prevalence of this essential tendency. Associations of sounds are also visible (and audible) in the varied and unpredictable rhyming patterns used by Corbière. Some rhymes are conventional, but many are aberrant, or gratuitous, including homonyms, "illegal" hyphenation (*-of/-loff*, in "La Balancelle"), phonic alterations ("Turcs/truc," in the same poem), visual rhymes ("fils/fils" and "Aïeule/feuille," in "La Rapsode foraine et le pardon de Sainte-Anne"). It is interesting to note that Verlaine, in his *Les Poètes maudits*, passes this off as a pardonable imperfection, placing Corbière in the same category as other "only human" poets like Homer, Goethe, and Shakespeare(!):

As a rimer and a prosodist, he's not impeccable, that is to say dull. Not one among the Greats like him is impeccable, from Homer who dozes from time to time, to the very human Goethe (whatever they say about him), by way of the more than irregular Shakespeare. The impeccable poets, these are . . . such and such.

Associations of words, in which specific expressions, or even images, seem to summon up similar ones, are also used by Corbière to give the reader an impression of spontaneity. Since it is a more complex technique, we would do better not to give desultory examples selected at random from his poetry. Rather, let us see how it works, in concert with some of the other techniques mentioned above, in one of Corbière's most brilliant poems, "Litanie du sommeil." It is here that we see the supreme paradox—*the development and careful use of techniques which reflect spontaneity and freedom from control.*

## VI  *The "Litany of Slumber"*

"Litanie du sommeil," in many ways unique in the context of *Les Amours jaunes*, presents a problem to the critic (and reader) of Corbière's poetry. It is one of the few extremely long poems in the volume. (The others are "Le Poète contumace," "La Rapsode foraine et le pardon de Sainte-Anne," and "Le bossu Bitor.") It is, more important, a poem which, like Corbière in his epoch, defies categorization, admittedly (according to the title of the section in which it appears), a *raccroc*, a "fluke." Outside the boundaries of the traditionally viewed dichotomy in Corbière's work, i.e., "poems of Paris" and "poems of Brittany," it is also the only oneiric poem Corbière ever attempted. Ironically, it was regarded by the Surrealists as typical of his interest in dream-literature and was thus the source of their interest in him. In *Les Amours jaunes*, it stands apart, moreover (along with the six *Rondels pour après*), as a journey to a world outside the oppressive "real" one and thus may be considered as one of the rare examples of "escape literature" in Corbière's poetry. So many motifs are fused in the text, and the major thrust of the poem is so multifaceted, that its treatment by critics is consequently varied and even, unsurprisingly, contradictory. For example, Corbière's attitude toward slumber has been viewed as both seductive and supplicating, and the interpretation of the function of sleep has varied from hope and salvation to a kind of premature death. Perhaps as a result of some or all of these factors, a detailed analysis of the poem has yet to be undertaken.

Before examining in what ways the poetic techniques used in "Litanie du sommeil" are characteristically Corbiérian, we should first take a brief look at what the poem is all about. The poet begins by interrogating a personage which he names "RUMINANT" ("one who ruminates" or "fodder-chewer"). In the context of the opening stanza, the latter clearly represents the typical bourgeois husband, lying (and snoring) next to his wife in a dumb stupor. (There is a subsequent allusion to "casques-à-meche honnêtes," "honest night-caps.") To the poet's question of whether he has ever experienced insomnia, the answer—supplied by the poet, since the "RUMI-NANT" is, of course, in a dead sleep—is in the negative. What is implied throughout most of the remainder of the lengthy text, then, is that because he can't know insomnia, the "RUMINANT" (a paradigm for "ordinary" people) can't know "Sommeil," or the anticipation of it, in its deepest form. And this is what occupies nearly the entire text, as the poet describes the wonderful, strange, sometimes terrifying universe of Slumber which the active (implied: poetic) imagination is capable of conjuring up. An avalanche of images is evoked to describe this obsessive phenomenon, including allusions to the worlds of humans, animals, flowers, inanimate objects, the elements, music, poetry, journalism, religion, fairy tales, and mythology. At the conclusion of this dazzling litany, the poet again addresses the "RUMINANT," this time concluding—always rhetorically, since the latter is still dormant—that not only are insomnia and true Slumber out of reach, but, as a result, so is "Le Réveil" (Awakening"). This is (again, with the *Rondels pour après*) the only text in *Les Amours jaunes* in which the conflict between the poet and others results in a dualism which presents the former in the light of hope and fulfillment and the latter as a negative force (i.e., the ironic self-flagellations so prevalent elsewhere have vanished). This direct expression of "good" (the poet) and "bad" (the "RUMINANT") is much more typical of a poet like Charles Cros, whose imaginative fantasies were created to counteract the unhappiness inflicted on the poet's sensitive soul by the typical bourgeois.

It is essential not to allow the questions which surround this text to obscure the extraordinary use of language exhibited in it. These questions range from whether the insomnia (like the question of deafness in "Rapsodie du sourd") is autobiographical or fictive to whether the function of the visions is psychic or cathartic, liberating or obsessive, optimistic or fatalistic. Rather than speculate on these problems, let us proceed to an examination of the dominating aspect of the text—the uninhibited and monumental exhibition of poetic technique.

What is immediately apparent is that there is a perfect correspondence between form and content: the litany of visions is expressed in a manner with which Corbière feels totally comfortable and which we may term his "style of accumulation." Because the first-person perspective and ironic tone are absent, the language itself seems more autonomous than that used in Corbière's other poems, but many of the facets of the "Corbiérian lyre" we have been discussing are nevertheless quite visible. Because the poem is so immense, it will not be possible to discuss every passage; for our purposes, however, the citation of a passage which appears in the exact middle of the poem should suffice:

> SOMMEIL—Écoute-moi, je parlerai bien bas:
> Crépuscule flottant de l'*Être ou n'Être pas*! . . .
>
> SOMBRE lucidité! Clair-obscur! Souvenir
> De l'Inouï! Marée! Horizon! Avenir!
> Conte des *Mille-et-une-nuits* doux à ouïr!
> Lampiste d'*Aladin* qui sais nous éblouir!
> Eunuque noir! muet blanc! Derviche! Djinn! Fakir!
> Conte de Fée où *le Roi* se laisse assoupir!
> Forêt-vierge où *Peau-d'Âne* en pleurs va s'accroupir!
> Garde-manger où l'*Ogre* encor va s'assouvir!
> Tourelle où *ma soeur Anne* allait voir rien venir!
> Tour où *dame Malbrouck* voyait page courir . . .
> Où *Femme Barbe-Bleue* oyait l'heure mourir! . . .
> Où *Belle-au-Bois-Dormant* dormait dans un soupir!

SLUMBER—I'll speak softly, listen to me:
Floating dusk of *To be or not To be!* . . .

SOMBER lucidity! Chiaroscuro! Memory's tie
With the unheard of! Tide! Horizon! Future well-nigh!
Tale of *1001 Nights* pleasant to my
Ear! *Aladdin's* lamp-lighter who can make us high!
Black eunuch! white mute! Djinn! Fakir! Dervish whirling by!
Fairy-tale where *The King* goes rock-a-bye!
Virgin-forest where *Peau d'Âne* goes to crouch and cry!
Pantry where the *Ogre* still goes to self-satisfy!
Turret where *my sister Anne* went to see nothing come by!
Tower where *Lady Malbrouck* saw the page run by . . .
Where *Lady Blue-Beard* heard the hour die! . . .
Where *Sleeping Beauty* was sleeping with a sigh!

The traits characteristic of the entire text which we see here are
several. They are similar to those in other poems, but whereas in
the latter cases they are employed consciously to "depoeticize" the
text, in "Litanie du sommeil" they are, rather, consistent with the
evocation of an unconscious, frenetic state of mind. In terms of
physical appearance on the page, punctuation and lettering function
to achieve this end. Although the dash is used frequently elsewhere
in the poem, in this passage the exclamation point (and, to a lesser
degree, the ellipses) help to express the fantastic and frenetic nature
of the universe of SLUMBER. That almost all of the verses end with
an exclamation point is not surprising in the context of the poem
(this phenomenon occurs in 117 of the total 164 verses); the nine
internal exclamation points also contribute to the fragmentation of
the nocturnal visions. This fragmentation can also be noted in the
unequal length of stanzas, totally chaotic to reflect this element of
the poem's visions, and which range from one to sixteen verses. The
sporadic vehemence of the expression of these visions is effected, in
part, by the use of capital letters and italics.

In regard to the "style of accumulation" so essential to the dizzy-
ing array of images (it is, after all, a *litany*), in this passage we see
three basic techniques which Corbière controls skillfully throughout
the entire poem. One unifying thread which runs through these
rather disparate series of visions is the monorhyme, or the use of a
single rhyme throughout the whole stanza. This is the pattern for
almost the entire poem and is not as easy to produce as we might

suspect. Another is the use of parallel constructions. It is important to note that Corbière's use of this device—usually in the form of anaphora, or the repetition of the same expression at symmetrical points of a verse or consecutive verses—is never static or simply for emphasis, but rather, varied and shifting, to reflect the movement and heterogeneity of the visions in question. Most obvious is the beginning of nine of the first ten verses with a substantive which is each time a metaphor for SOMMEIL. In fact, most of the poem is concerned with this very transformation of slumber into its various, seemingly endless visionary representations. In vv. 7–8 of the above passage, the parallel construction is in the form of hyphenated expressions, "Forêt-vierge" and "Garde-manger," the first acting as an imaginary springboard for the second. Since there are no apparent "logical" links between the two, they are bound by ties which are purely orthographic, hence fantastic. In the two verses which follow, the links between images ("Tourelle," "Tour") become linguistic and semantic. And in the final two verses, we see an orthodox use of anaphora in the repetition of "Où." Corbière has not finished, however: there are, in addition, various *internal* parallels in the stanza. The italics serve to link the various allusions to folklore and fairytale; the relative "où" is repeated internally in vv. 6–10; the combination "va" + reflexive infinitive ("s'accroupir," "s'assouvir") appears in vv. 7–8; and the switch to the imperfect tense (followed by direct object and infinitive) links vv. 10–11 ("voyait page courir," "oyait l'heure mourir").

A third technique so essential to "Litanie du sommeil" is antithesis, the juxtaposition of two opposite expressions. Unlike Baudelaire's "pillow of evil," for example, the function of Corbière's antithesis is not figurative, but tautological: the coexistence of opposite phenomena is not only permitted, but, in the oneiric context of the poem, is actually the conceptual basis of Corbière's imagery. The examples found in this passage—the chiasmic "SOMBRE lucidité! Clair-obscur" and "Eunuque noir! muet blanc!"—are surrounded, in other passages, by many, many more: "Roulette de fortune / De tout infortuné" ("Fortune-wheel / Of luckless ones"), "CUIRASSE du petit! Camisole du fort!" ("BREAST-PLATE of the small! Strait-jacket of the strong"), "BOULET des forcenés, Liberté des captifs!" ("BALL-AND-CHAIN of the frenzied, Freedom of the prisoners!"), "Actif du passif et Passif de l'actif!" ("Active of the passive and Passive of the active"), "Du jeune homme rêveur Sin-

gulier Féminin! / De la femme rêvant pluriel masculin!" ("Feminine
Singular of the dreamy young man! / Masculine plural of the
dreaming woman!"), "Faux du vrai! Vrai du faux!" ("False of the
true! True of the false!"), and so on.

. This technique of antithesis brings us to the most outstanding
feature of "Litanie du sommeil"—its imagery. Almost all the images
in the poem are simply metaphors in apposition with "SOMMEIL";
their function is to express the marvelous, fantastic universe of
slumber. In this (poetic) state, everything is possible: opposites
coexist, the sick are healed, the mute becomes prophet, incoher-
ence is understood, thieves become honest, prisoners are set free,
the disgraced find grace, etc. Furthermore, many of the images,
although in apposition with "SOMMEIL," have little or nothing to
do with it; consequently, the reader is left with a feeling of disorientation. Instead of clarifying the phenomenon of slumber, they appear to obfuscate its true nature and to plunge the poem into the
realm of the arbitrary. This autonomy of imagery is generally the
center of attention in critical discussions of "Litanie du sommeil," as
the following comment by Michel Dansel indicates:

Corbière, as we know, refuses to control his language: he willingly allows
himself to be submerged by it, or more precisely he leaves the words the
power of evoking new images, unorthodox couplings. This process of writing permits him to say all and confers to his work a freedom of expression
which was, until then, rarely attained.[9]

But this assertion is arguable, if we read the poem carefully and in
the light of what we now know to be Corbière's writing process. For
even in such a seemingly arbitrary poem in which the barrage of
images seems to be running wild, the familiar Corbiérian paradox is
still operative: the tempering of chaos with control, of spontaneity
with structure.

Although the Surrealists applauded this poem as a true precursor
of their art (i.e., the images therein were perceived as being "automatic," uncontrolled), its author is not really submerged by the
images; as with his manipulations of sound, meaning, grammar, and
syntax we discussed in the passage cited above, Corbière *does* control his language and, in fact (and as always), revels in it. Paradoxically, this poem about the world of dreams and the unconscious is
less "about" the visions invoked than the language which expresses

these visions. And that is why we can call "Litanie du sommeil" a poem and not just a long recital of imagined items.

Let us examine, first, how Corbière unifies this enormously chaotic text in general, and then how, in the opening passages, he delights in manipulating and controlling specific images. On the level of the subject, "SOMMEIL" seems to be an ever-changing chameleon, flitting from one transformation to another. On the level of language, however, Corbière unifies his text with recurring motifs. If we follow the motif of the woman, for instance, we see that it first appears in stanza 1 and then reappears in stanzas 3 ("vierges," "virgins"), 4 ("l'Aimée," "the Beloved"), 7 ("Femme," "Woman"), 12 ("Maîtresse," "Mistress"), 15 ("femme-forte," "strong-woman"), and so on. Other recurrent subjects are water ("mer," "sea"; "tempêtes," "tempests"; "Vaisseau," "Vessel"; "FONTAINE," "noyer," "au large," "FOUNTAIN," "drown," "on the open sea"), in stanzas 1, 3, 7, and 10; fairytales, in stanzas 4, 14, and 18; wind (5, 14, 25), and mythology (20, 25, 28). Many other items reappear once (e.g., voices, insects, strings, light, genies, animals), demonstrating that the balance between automatism and control is constantly maintained in the poem's imagery.

A concrete example of "image-manipulation" occurs in the poem's opening four stanzas. "RUMINANT," the metaphor for the bovine sleeper (v. 2), is followed by the curious "pot-au-noir" ("black-pot") in which he sleeps. There seems to be no connection between the two images, but if we hypothesize that the genesis of the word *pot-au-noir* may have been the more familiar *pot-au-feu* (a sort of boiled *beef* dish), Corbière's ludic (thus, for him, poetic) intent becomes apparent. The adjective "ailé" ("winged") which modifies "Sommeil" in v. 3 is soon followed by both the apposition "Papillon de minuit" ("Midnight butterfly") and the phrase "Sans un coup d'aile ami" ("Without a friendly flutter": the "aile" is substituted for the usual *coup de main*, "[to give] a hand"). "Pensée" ("thought") in v. 7 leads to "tête" ("head"), which (roundly) evokes both "boule" ("ball") and "ballon" ("balloon"). Finally, "chandelles," the strange flickering candles seen by the insomniac, are followed, in stanza 3, by the "casques-à-mèche" ("sleeping caps"), a compound word ending with the word for "wick," "mèche."

In stanza 3, "Oreiller" ("Pillow") precedes "Matelas" ("Mattress"); and, in a more desultory reference, "Proxénète" ("Procuror"), in apposition to "SOMMEIL," evokes, twenty-one verses later, another appositional phrase, "Femme du rendez-vous" ("Shady lady"). And, in an extremely distant repetition, the "Sac noir" ("Black bag"), a metaphor for "SOMMEIL," reappears in the final verse of the poem (v. 163), this time as "Sac ensommeillé" ("Sleepy bag"), a description of the "RUMINANT." We should notice, in passing, that this "framing" of the poem with references to the "RUMINANT"—otherwise absent throughout—is further evidence of Corbière's consciousness of form in a poem which *seems* not to have any.

In the fourth stanza, word-pairs continue to evolve. We see, for example, "gris/Noir" ("gray/Black"), "Loup-Garou/Loup de velours" ("Werewolf/Velvet night-mask," a typical pun), and "Cendrillon" ("Cinderella"), perhaps evoked by the Wolf, who also appears, of course, in another fairytale, Little-Red-Riding-Hood. Finally, "Voleur de nuit" ("Night-thief") precedes "Honnêteté des voleurs" ("Honesty of thieves"), which appears thirty-six verses later. In short, word-play, parallel construction, and repetition of theme contribute, sometimes rather subtly, to the unity and coherence of a poem which expresses the most ununified and incoherent of subjects imaginable. Just how subtle Corbière's poetry is (without appearing as such) we shall discover in the pages to follow.

## CHAPTER 3

# Poet or Prankster?: Corbière's Oblique Aesthetics

## I  A Bagful of Pranks

AS readers of Corbière's poetry, we are confronted with a special problem: if we are supposed to take poetry seriously—and none of us should doubt that we should—what are we to make of the endless barrage of jokes, pranks, and general trickery which our poet perpetrates? Is this a poet writing, or a vaudeville comedian with his bag of one-liners, a magician with his rabbits, a fool like Gilbert and Sullivan's Jack Point, trained in the art of comedy and using his gags like a shroud over his broken heart? We shall attempt to find a solution during the course of the pages to follow, but for the moment let us take a closer look at what is inside his bag of tricks.

Corbière's presentation of himself as "nonpoet" is a constant one, and his attempt to confound, surprise, and dazzle the reader is everywhere apparent. In fact, even his selection of the Glady Bros. press, which catered to readers of pornography, still raises the eyebrows of "dignified" people. It underscores his unorthodox aversion to, and lack of concern for, the notions of success and publication for fame and profit so predominant in the positivistic, industrial, bourgeois milieu of post–Franco-Prussian War France.

The very presentation of many of his poems, i.e., the "trappings" of title, epigraph, and subscription (what we might call the "peritext"), is disconcerting, even bewildering. Generally, poem titles function either as résumés of an action or a condition to be described in the body of the text; as opaque statements of motifs, protagonists, or spatial or temporal settings; as metaphorical representations of the poem's ambiance or general thrust; and so on. Epigraphs and subscriptions usually serve to increase the poem's poignancy with

61

extratextual allusions, or to situate it in time or place, respectively. These notations surrounding the poem are rarely autonomous, but, ancillary to the text, depend entirely on it for meaning, functioning, without independent aesthetic value, as signposts which direct the reader forward or backward to the main attraction, the poem itself. Occasionally, a poet's consistent practice will deviate from this time-honored pattern. At one pole of usage stands Mallarmé, supreme Poet, whose conscious neglect of peri-textual phenomena (particularly titles: a bit more than two-fifths of his "mature" poems are untitled) was intended to create a visible void, part of the "vide papier que la blancheur défend" ("empty paper defended by whiteness"), the whiteness of the page which would suspend the text rather than subordinate it, as a title would do. At the opposite end of the spectrum is Corbière, supreme Nonpoet, whose ludic treatment of these phenomena *as poetic techniques* is essential to his own self-expression and to the understanding of his literary pose by the perceptive reader.

The Corbiérian title manifests varying degrees of unorthodoxy. Of the some 100 poems in the collection, only eighteen include articles preceding the substantive. More significant, however, are those texts which reflect a particular type of nose-thumbing at the conventional title. In one case, a Roman numeral is used instead of the definite article ("I Sonnet"), and one title is followed by unexpectedly excited punctuation ("Hidalgo!"). Four are in Italian ("Veder Napoli poi mori," "Elizir d'amor," "Libertà," "Soneto a Napoli"), and two are in English ("Steam-Boat," "À mon chien Pope—gentleman-dog from New-land—mort d'une balle"). It is noteworthy that portions of three of these titles are (willfully, as always) imprecise: "Veder(. . .)mori" for "Vedi(. . .)muori," "Elizir d'amor" for "Elisir d'amor(e)," and "New-land" for "Newfoundland." We also find abbreviation ("Vésuves et C$^{ie}$"), neologism ("Décourageux"), pun ("Nature morte," meaning "still-life" or, literally, "dead nature"), and archaism ("Gente dame").

More consistently perpetrated on the conditioned reader of that time are the deviations of lengthy and detailed (sub-)titles and those which include special qualifications. In the first category, we find: "Soneto a Napoli. All'solo, all'luna, all'sabato, all'canonico è tutti quanti. Con Pulcinella," "La Complaincte morlaisienne. Ousque sont habillés [*sic*] en grande tenue les édilités et autres et mis sur l'air de Fualdès par le sieur Corbière Édouard et ousque sont apostillées et soulignées les plus espirituelles choses pour le plus grand esbastement des obstus d'esprit—," "Cap'taine Ledoux. À la bonne relâche des caboteurs, veuve-cap'taine Galmiche, chaudière pour les marins—Cook-house Brandy—Liqœur—Pouliage," "Le Douanier. Elégie de corps-de-garde. A la mémoire des douaniers gardes-côtes mis à la retraite le 30 novembre 1869," "Véritable complainte d'Auguste Berthelon, mort à l'art fin courant sur l'air de . . . dans sa villa San Crepina (route de Paris)," "Ode aux Déperrier par M. de Malherbe sur les émanations de l'écurie du rez-de-chaussée et les tuyaux du second, maison Corbière n°38," and "Les Pannoïdes ou les trois mystères du greffier Panneau, savoir: 1° les fiançailles 2° la conception 3° l'enfantement." (The final three appear in *Poèmes retrouvés*.) The qualifying subtitles playfully answer the unposed questions "how?" ("I Sonnet, avec la manière de s'en servir"), "who?" ("À la mémoire de Zulma, vierge-folle hors barrière et d'un louis," "À mon chien Pope—gentleman-dog from New-Land —mort d'une balle"), "where?" ("Libertà. A la cellule IV *bis* [prison royale de Gênes]"), and, in *Poèmes divers*, "when?" ("Sous un portrait de Corbière en couleurs fait par lui et daté de 1868").

Tristan's penchant to confuse and confound is reflected in his frequent epigraphs. We have already mentioned (in chapter 1) the long, incoherent epigraph to "Épitaphe" taken from the apocryphal "Sagesse des nations." Perhaps it is even significant that the equation of "beginning" and "end" may be applied to one type of Corbiérian notation, which seems to appear indiscriminately as epigraph and as subscription. This is his allusion to places and dates, many of which are so unspecific as to be useless to the reader. Examples appearing as epigraphs include "Avril" ("Idylle coupée"), "Bougival, 8 mai" ("À la mémoire de Zulma"), "Bois de Boulogne, 1er mai" ("Déjeuner de soleil"), and "La Vera-Cruz, 10 février" ("Lettre du Mexique"). Foreign languages appear not only in the poems, but on top of them as well. Corbière uses Italian with a willed pedantry in two poems, in which the epigraphs add virtually nothing to the total impact: "*Morire*" in "Un jeune qui s'en va" and "*Odor della feminità*" in "Bonne fortune et fortune." The same is true for his use of Latin, in "À un Juvénal de lait": "*Incipe, parve puer, risu cognoscere . . . [matrem].*" The latter is an allusion to Vergil's fourth *Bucolic*, and the incongruous citation of "refined" literature preceding texts which are anything but that is typical of other devices of incongruity which are part of Corbière's arsenal in the poems themselves.[1] Other examples, taken from, again, the fourth *Bucolic*, Vergil's *Georgics*, II, Dante, and (twice) Shakespeare, respectively, are as follows: *"Sicelides Musae, paulo majora canamus"* ("À l'Etna"), *"O fortunatos nimium, sua si . . ."* ("Un riche en Bretagne"), *"Lasciate ogni . . ."* ("Libertà"), *"What? . . ."* ("Ça?"), and *"J'ai scié le sommeil—MACBETH"* (a parody of Act 2, Scene 2, in "Litanie du sommeil"). The ludic element is most obvious in the latter two, which represent one of the Bard's least memorable (and most truncated) quotes, and a "Shakespeare in translation." Citations are also pilfered from a François Bazin operetta ("Quand l'on fut toujours vertueux/L'on aime à voir lever l'aurore," in "Aurora") and Lamartine's *Graziella* (a rather long passage, with a pricetag ironically appended—I fr.25c. le vol.—in "Le Fils de Lamartine et de Graziella"). Finally, two curious tendencies are the repetition of the identical epigraph (*"La Bête féroce,"* "the ferocious Beast," a sarcastic reference to Woman), in "Femme" and "Pauvre garçon"; and the reference to an undetermined addressee in "Rapsodie du sourd" (*"À Madame D***"*) and "Steam-Boat" (*À une passagère"*).

Even more bizarre are the subscriptions appended to nearly half the poems in *Les Amours jaunes* (in all, forty-eight). Almost all of these are places and dates which are imaginary, imagined, or otherwise outlandish or undependable. This is yet another source of the abortiveness of the efforts of those critics who attempt to track down solutions to enigmas or lacunae by using biographical details as evidence. One critic has even stated that of all the places and dates mentioned by Corbière, only *four* were real or at least credible.[2] Speculation or not, this type of "fact" only corroborates the literary shenanigans that this practice reflects in Corbière. Among the many places never frequented by Tristan, but which he pretends were the sites of the writing of various poems, are "Préfecture de police" ("Ça?"), "Jérusalem" ("Bohème de chic"), and "Cellule 4 *bis.*— Genova-la-Superba" ("Libertà"). Some dates are patently ludicrous: most omit either the year, the day of the month, or, in one case, both month and day ("1870," in "La Pastorale de Conlie"). The day of the week is replaced by an unhelpful demonstrative, in "Le Crapaud" ("Ce soir, 20 Juillet"). Place names or locations are often even more ludicrous. They include "10' long.0./40' lat.N." ("Steam-Boat"), "British channel.—15 may" ("Sonnet à Sir Bob"), "Méditerranée" ("Décourageux"), (*"Lits divers—Une nuit de jour"*) ("Litanie du sommeil"), and "À bord" ("La Goutte," "La Fin").

Further evidence of Corbière's pose as dilettante (the opposite of the "serious Poet") is in four subscriptions written in Italian (following "Veder Napoli poi mori," "Vésuves et C^{ie}," "Soneto a Napoli," and "Le Fils de Lamartine et de Graziella") and one in Spanish (following "Hidalgo!"). In one (following "Pudentiane"), Corbière states his age as forty (he died at twenty-nine). The subscription of "À la mémoire de Zulma" ("Saint-Cloud.—Novembre.") contradicts the information given in the epigraph ("Bougival, 8 mai"). Appended to "Le Poète contumace" is "Penmarc'h—jour de Noël." Here, the "fake" Tristan is playfully (painfully?) appropriating the site of the suicide of the "real" one, the Tristan of legend. (The same site is alluded to after the conclusion of the prose piece, *Casino des trépassés.*) And heading the list of "non-subscriptions" are the three asterisks which curiously follow "Femme," "Fleur d'art," and "Pauvre garçon."

Precursor of a certain type of modernity in the poetry of the present century, Corbière, through his poetic innovations, particularly those of a lexical and formal nature, clearly exerted an extraordinary influence on many of his successors, notably Pound and Eliot. What should now be apparent as well is that this purely ludic use of peri-textual phenomena, which occurs in his verse for the first time (with any regularity) in the French lyric tradition, has also been taken up by later poets. We can cite as examples, among many, the epigraphs of Laforgue and the titles of Jacob, Éluard, and Leiris. In this respect, however, Corbière was more than a precursor: his use of the peri-text was unique in that, perhaps for the only time in the tradition of French verse, its role in regard to the "voice" of the poet, and to his presentation of himself to the reader, was consistent and integral.

Corbière's penchant for mischief and willed confusion is evident not only in his use of language and the presentation of individual poems, but also in the structure and general presentation of *Les Amours jaunes* as a whole. The collection is composed of seven sections: the brief section entitled *Ça*, followed by *Les Amours jaunes, Sérénade des Sérénades, Raccrocs, Armor, Gens de mer*, and *Rondels pour après*. These sections can be divided (almost too conveniently) into two separate parts, the first four sections corresponding to the themes of Corbière's (unrequited and jaundiced) love for Marcelle, Paris, and the poet's isolation; and the latter three to the theme of Brittany and its inhabitants, topology, religion, and mythology. The first four titles are typically ironic: *Ça* reflects the anonymity of the poet and his verse in a hostile Parisian milieu; Tristan's loves are not blue or red, but yellow *(Les Amours jaunes)*; the parodies of (among others, Musset's) "Spanish" poetry are referred to as *Sérénade des Sérénades,* a perversion of the biblical *Cantique des Cantiques ("Song of Songs");* and the various poems in the fourth section are but *raccrocs,* or "flukes." By contrast, the titles of sections 5–7 are serious and descriptive, having deep emotional value for the poet: *Armor* is the Celtic name for his native Brittany; *Gens de mer* are the sailors, the fishermen, the deformed souls, in short, the inhabitants of the region; and *Rondels pour après* solemnly announces the posthumous lullabies to follow. Aside from the divergence in titles, the two divisions can be differentiated further by a clear change of tone. The first four sections are much more self-directed, ironic, and negative; in the final three, the "pranks" diminish quite a bit, and the first person nearly disappears, replaced by a clearly objective point of view which is more positive in its outlook.

It all seems to fall into place. Poems of Paris, poems of Brittany, negative Tristan, positive Corbière: a clear evolution. Furthermore, two little poems—similar parodies of La Fontaine's fable (with titles reversed) entitled "Le Poète et la cigale" and "La Cigale et le Poète" and both dedicated "À Marcelle"—frame the entire volume, giving further unity to its structure. Easy, right? Wrong! As always, what *seems* to be clear deserves further examination. If we look more closely, we shall see that this unity is only another pose and disguises what is really relative confusion.

A series of questions, probably unanswerable (perhaps only Tristan knew, must now be posed. Regarding the "framing" poems to Marcelle, does this not undermine the unity of the volume, by shifting the emphasis entirely to the themes of sections 1–4? If so, why the pretense of uniting the entire volume? The establishment of a thematic hierarchy and the consideration of Paris and Brittany as two parts of a dialectic are thus hopelessly contradictory. In this regard, does not the very title *Les Amours jaunes* also orient the volume as a whole toward the theme of love, again devaluing the presence of Brittany?

Even more enigmatic is the chronology of *Les Amours jaunes.* When was each poem written? As we have mentioned, Corbière leaves the dates of composition a mystery in most cases by falsifying them. There is, then, no chronological pattern. The arrangement of sections in the definitive edition of *Les Amours jaunes* is also a mystery. Thanks to critics like Martineau, Le Dantec, and Sonnenfeld, the dates of composition of the various sections can be approximated: *Gens de mer* and *Armor* were probably composed between 1868–71, *Les Amours jaunes, Sérénade des Sérénades,* and *Raccrocs* between 1872–73, and, finally, the *Rondels pour après* in 1873. The question which these dates evoke, then, is "why did Corbière arrange the sections with no concern for chronology?" Why not at least place the *Rondels pour après* first so that there would be at least a consistent "backwards" order of composition? In fact, in one section, *Gens de mer* (if we can believe the dates given), there *is* a backwards chronology: beginning with "Lettre du Mexique" and continuing to the end of the section, the dates attributed to poems are, in order, May-December-November-November-August-May-February. Some, like Sonnenfeld, see in this arrangement a symbolic (not chronological) progression from the negative, ironic poems to a positive acceptance of native Brittany and, in the *Rondels pour après,* the peace of death. Others, like Ida Levi, see total chaos:

It seems quite impossible to talk of a preconceived structure of the book. The individual parts of *Les Amours jaunes* do not acquire any particular significance if read in the order in which they were printed—they do not have any internal development of thought, nor, on the other hand, do they change or convey a different meaning if read in another order. The six parts are, in a sense, autonomous and independent; each could form a separate book.[3]

Although the first judgment is more credible, there are too many internal inconsistencies in each section (e.g., the placement of "Litanie du sommeil"), in addition to the other problems of structure, to permit us to be certain of such a conscious and orderly development. The confusion of the reader is too much a part of Corbière's poetic strategy to allow for such coherence. We have only to compare *Les Amours jaunes* to the volumes of Hugo, Rimbaud, Mallarmé, and especially Baudelaire to see this deviation from the established norm of some progression or development, either chronological or thematic.

## II  *"Not Poetry, Not Verse, Hardly Literature"*

Corbière's desire to leave the (false) impression that he was no poet was wildly successful, making easy victims of so many critics and readers who have consented to take him at his word. Names as illustrious as Bloy, Gourmont, and Le Goffic have accepted his lack of sophistication, absence of aesthetic concern, and unorthodoxy at face value, consequently regarding our poet as nothing more than what he advertised himself as: a jokester, a crackpot, a naïf. Corbière *as poet* has received (until very recently) less than serious consideration, and the subtlety and ambiguity of his verse has been largely over- (under-?) looked. Probably the greatest culprit in this regard was Corbière's contemporary, the great Uruguayan-born French poet, Jules Laforgue (1860–87). Although he has some lucid judgments of Corbière's psychological motives for employing certain techniques, his criticism of the Breton poet is to a great extent a reflection of his own poetic self-consciousness. Laforgue fancied himself an aesthete (some would term this tendency "decadent"), a "serious" poet; and when he read Léo Trézenik's review of his own *Les Complaintes* in the journal *Lutèce* (9–16 April 1885), comparing his verse to Corbière's, he could scarcely believe his eyes. The response to Trézenik, a letter written in August, 1885, and appearing in *Lutèce* on 4 October, is a model of defensive counterattack:

Everyone throws Corbière up at me. Let me tell you for the record that my *Complaintes* were at Vanier's six months before the publication of [Verlaine's] *Poètes maudits* and that I obtained the volume of *Les Amours jaunes* only last June (a rare copy purchased at Vanier's). So, I recognize a grain of parentage with the adorable and irreparable loon Corbière(. . .)Corbière has gadgets and I, humor; Corbière flutters and I purr; I live by an absolute philosophy and not by tics; I am accessible and not deceptively frisky; my love is not yellow, but white and deep mourning purple. Finally, Corbière is concerned with neither stanza nor rhymes (save as a springboard for conceits) and never with rhythms, and I preoccupy myself with them to the point of conceiving new stanzas, rhymes, and rhythms; my goals are symphony and melody, and Corbière saws away on that confounded fiddle.[4]

Even more critical of Corbière's (non-) aesthetics are Laforgue's notes, published as "Une Étude sur Corbière," which appeared in the review *Entretiens politiques et littéraires* in 1891. After calling Corbière "falot" ("grotesque" or "gay") and "inculte" ("uncultivated"), Laforgue casts further aspersions:

—Without an aesthetics—All, and above all Corbière—but not poetry, not verse, hardly literature. (. . .)—not an art but a manner—A very-chic appearance not a profound aesthetics(. . .)He's not an artist(. . .)he has a trade without plastic interest—the interest, the effect is in the daft, the dry-point, the pun, the frisky remark, the jerky Romantic style. He's cramped in the verse—he abounds in—in!in. . .in parentheses,—in monosyllables.—not one verse can be singled out as poetically beautiful—nothing but what is curious in form.

Tics, tricks, *chic*, squeak . . . but no poetry, no "plastic" interest. It is now time to come to Tristan's defense, to determine whether, besides being a prankster, he was a poet as well.

It seems all too clear that, just as Rimbaud noted that Baudelaire's one flaw was to have written in "too artistic a milieu," so Laforgue's aestheticism obscured for him what may be called Corbière's "aesthetics of antipoetry." It was precisely this plastic art, stiff and formal, cluttered with rules, and stifling to the expression of real experience which Corbière attempted to deform; the idea of the poetic artisan (Gautier's "Sculpte, lime, cisèle," "Sculpt, file, chisel," defines this "Parnassian" trait) who took an inert model and refined it with his poetic tools so that no excess or waste remained was, quite simply, repulsive to Corbière. The excessive concern for plasticity minimized the affective value of the poem itself (quite the opposite of Romantic poets who were by and large unconcerned with technique) and was viewed by our poet as dishonest.

Before examining Corbière's replacement of one poetic system for another, we should consider three important points which might clarify the justification of Corbière as poet. First, it is certain that, although with less assiduity than other, "serious" poets, he did make corrections of original versions of various poems.[5] The alteration of the original manuscripts of *Les Amours jaunes* in 1874, even after their publication, reflects a desire to refine, considered essential by most critics as a necessary element of *poesis*. Second, he *did*, after all, publish his verse, even if his poetry is perceived merely as a sublimation of his lived frustrations and failures. It is entirely possible that if he had been robust and healthy, he might have become a sailor and nothing else (opting, as Rimbaud did after a curiously brief literary career, for "life on the open road"); and, if he had written poetry, it surely would have been entirely different from the verse he in fact produced. It is a commonplace that experience is the lifeblood of literature, and, as in Proust's case as well (but how differently!), the experience of physical disfunction can profoundly affect what is written. But the fact remains that Corbière was not forced to write or to publish, if not by some inner motivation to do so. The late American poetess Anne Sexton put it eloquently, and her statement about drives which need no explanation can be applied to Corbière's situation as a poet:

> But suicides have a special language.
> Like carpenters they want to know *which tools.*
> They never ask *why build.*[6]

Finally, the contention that Corbière was only capable of "tics" and afflicted with bad grammar, bad spelling, and little knowledge of correct prosody because of a lack of culture or literary background is simply not plausible. On the contrary, he was widely read (the learned citations in his epigraphs and elsewhere attest to this), had a good background in modern and classical languages, and was well acquainted with the rules of French prosody, as Germain Delpuech suggests:

When he wants to, he knows all the resources of the language and of the verse, is classical in the use of the diphthong and of dieresis, handles the short verse with the grace of Charles d'Orléans. . .and achieves alliterations which are as clever as Mallarmé's.[7]

This statement, however, disregards the essential fact that on the whole (even though he *could*), Corbière did *not* wish to write "correctly" and, moreover, typifies the insidious critical tendency to compare Corbière's poetic language constantly to that of others. (Comparisons to poets from Villon to Baudelaire in critical studies seem almost mandatory or instinctual.)

What Laforgue and those who followed him refused to admit was that Corbière's "nonaesthetics" *is* his aesthetics and constitutes the most irreverent pose of all.[8] If Corbière is to be faulted, it is for his being ahead of his time, for wishing to make anything (going much further in some respects than Hugo, for instance)—not just what was deemed correct—suitable material for poetry. It is, after all, a question of relativity, or even semantics, for who is to judge what is "poetic" and what is not? Corbière was acutely aware of this problem and, in fact, makes a point of avoiding aesthetic labels. He refers to his work in the following manners: "honteux monstre de livre" ("La Cigale et le Poète"), "Poète, en dépit de ses vers," "Ses vers faux furent ses seuls vrais," "De l'âme,—et pas de violon" ("Épitaphe"), "C'était un poète à peu près" ("Une mort trop travaillée"), "mon drôle de livre," "Et je puis, par raccroc, qui sait, être un génie" (*"Donc, Madame, une nuit, un jour que j'étais ivre . . ."*). The expression "Art" is anathema: Corbière is an "Artiste sans art,—à l'envers" ("Épitaphe"); he is unacquainted with it in "Ça?" ("L'Art ne me connaît pas. Je ne connais pas l'Art"); and the doctor in "Rapsodie du sourd" is pejoratively referred to as "l'homme de l'art." The "Song" is to be avoided as well (the following are all perhaps oblique references to Banville's discussion of same in his *Petit traité de poésie française*): Tristan exclaims "Alors je chanterais (faux, comme de coutume)" ("Well, I'd sing [off-key, as usual]") in "Sous un portrait de Corbière," and in "Décourageux," he is a true poet, i.e., without a song ("Ce fut un vrai poète; Il n'avait pas de chant"). It is this last verse which most clearly illustrates Corbière's poetic perversion and perversity. The true poet has no literary baggage, no song, no "art." In fact, Corbière uses the word *poète* not to describe real poets, but ordinary people (like himself) who have poetry *inside* themselves. In "Matelots," the rugged sailors are described in this fashion: "à bord, chez eux, ils ont leur poésie!" ("On board, on their home territory, they have their poetry! "). In "Le Douanier," the customs official is a "Poète trop senti pour être poétique!" ("A poet too heartfelt to be poetic! "). Corbière is intentionally ambiguous in his attitude toward Poetry, and it is this subtle aspect which is most often misinterpreted or neglected. The reference to his verse as "a hit-or-miss affair, right or wrong, by chance . . .," for example, both denigrates a lack of reflection, of a plan in his poetry and implies that this very drawback constitutes the plan itself.

Corbière's "strangling of eloquence's neck" (even before Verlaine, who initiated the expression) was no freak, but a lucid venture. It is indeed ironic that this conscious substitution of discord (Laforgue's "crincrin"), apparent spontaneity, orality, in short, the pose of nonpoetry for *what was considered poetic* has so often been construed all too literally rather than as his own viable means of poetic expression. Those who seek an explicit aesthetic statement of aims in essays, letters, or *arts poétiques* will come up empty when dealing with Corbière. His aesthetics is, rather, oblique, implicit:

the innovation and complexity of his poetry, its subtle idiosyncrasies (and Corbière's consciousness of his own technical skills), often belie what seems to be a consistent artistic indifference and, in fact, themselves represent an implicit aesthetic code. This deception is nowhere more apparent than in "I Sonnet, avec la manière de s'en servir." Because it has been interpreted traditionally as a parody of the stiff Parnassian style (which it is, ostensibly), its importance as a capital text in which Corbière demonstrates his *own* poetics has been consistently overlooked.

### III   *The Muted Fiddle*

"De l'âme,—et pas de violon"
["Épitaphe"]

### I SONNET
#### AVEC LA MANIÈRE DE S'EN SERVIR

*Réglons notre papier et formons bien nos lettres:*

Vers filés à la main et d'un pied uniforme,
Emboîtant bien le pas, par quatre en peloton;
Qu'en marquant la césure, un des quatre s'endorme . . .
Ça peut dormir debout comme soldats de plomb.

Sur le *railway* du Pinde est la ligne, la forme;
Aux fils du télégraphe:—on en suit quatre, en long;
A chaque pied, la rime—exemple: *chloroforme.*
—Chaque vers est un fil, et la rime un jalon.

—Télégramme sacré—20 mots.—Vite à mon aide . . .
(*Sonnet—c'est un sonnet—*) ô Muse d'Archimède!
—La preuve d'un sonnet est par l'addition:

—Je pose 4 et 4 = 8! Alors je procède,
En posant 3 et 3!—Tenons Pégase raide:
"Ô lyre! Ô délire! Ô . . . "—Sonnet—Attention!

Pic de la Maladetta.—Août.

### I SONNET
#### AND HOW TO USE IT

*Let's put our paper in order and form our letters properly:*
Lines hand-crafted and with equal feet,
In perfect step, four in a bunch;
If, in marking the pause, one goes out to lunch . . .
Like standing lead soldiers it may fall asleep.

> On the Piṇdus *railway*, the line, the form;
> On telegraph wires:—we follow four, spread out;
> At each marker, the rhyme—example: *chloroform.*
> —Each verse is a wire, and the rhyme marks the route.
>
> Sacred telegram—20 words—Quick! give me some clues! . . .
> (Sonnet—it's a sonnet—) O Archimedes' Muse!
> The proof of a sonnet is by addition:
>
> —I add 4 and 4 = 8! And then I proceed,
> Adding 3 and 3!—Control that wingèd steed:
> "O lyre! O de-lyrium! O . . ."—Sonnet—Attention!

Taken literally (and not as a pose), "I Sonnet" is most obviously an *ars impoetica*, a poem literally about how *not* to write poetry. From the very start, we are given blatant hints that this is indeed Corbière's intent: from the use of the Roman numeral instead of the indefinite article in the title,[9] to the peremptory subtitle, to the epigraph directed to hypothetical schoolmarms ("*Réglons notre papier,*" etc.), to the truncated date appended to the poem, the humor of the parody is anything but hidden. An important point not yet considered, however, is that, contrary to the usual mode of parody, Corbière's criticism of Parnassian poetry is expressed *on his own terms.* Parody is normally effected by the exaggerated or distorted use of those very techniques or stylistic idiosyncrasies which characterize its target. In typical examples of parody of Parnassian models, for instance, the parodist generally (over)employs the descriptive techniques of his target (use of concrete description, especially of color and form; specific types of imagery; solemn or exotic vocabulary; classical and zoological allusions; and technical terminology), as in Charles Pornon's parody of Leconte de Lisle, "L'Exode des fourmis," and "Le Câble," a parody of Hérédia by Paul Reboux and Charles Müller.[10] In the "Dixains réalistes" which appear in the *Album Zutique* (as much pastiches as parodies), the approximate versification, stanzaic forms, and subject matter of the models are also used.[11] Such is not the case in "I Sonnet": as Corbière's own techniques, and not those of the Parnassians, are used, he is in effect posing once again. While appearing simply to parody the formalism of de Lisle and his group, he is at the same time presenting an *ars poetica* very different from more traditional ones: unlike Horace, Boileau, Gautier, and Verlaine (or even the Hugo of "Il faut que le poète . . ."), for example, Corbière presents his poetics not in theory, but in practice. It is not didactic, but rather a performance unaided by explanation. It is entirely consistent with his temperament in poetry as in life that he conceal the serious with the derisive; for just as he used humor and self-directed irony to conceal the basically tragic nature of his life, so in this sonnet his parodic treatment of an alien "school" of poetry hides the indirect statement—as direct a one as the irreverent Tristan was, in any case, capable of making—of his own method of writing.

As an oblique *ars poetica*, "I Sonnet" recommends, by "direct method," the use of many of Corbière's favorite "nonpoetic" techniques, just as the substance of the poem itself condemns traditional or "poetic" ones. The former usage is, of course, evident throughout his poetry, and it establishes him as one of the few French poets of the past century (along with, most notably, Rimbaud and Laforgue) whose linguistic innovations announced the subsequent revolution of poetic expression in the twentieth century, particularly in France and England. Even the subtitle of the sonnet may be construed as a Corbiérian pose: appearing to parody the utilitarian practice of sonnet-writing, it may also suggest—again indirectly—the *real* way (that is, Tristan's) of making use of the sonnet form.

The kinds of techniques used by Corbière in this pseudoparody (word associations, puns, etc.) appear at first to suggest that the creative act has been spontaneous, natural, unplanned—in short, the opposite of the regulated prosody perpetrated by "Le Parnasse." In fact, a look at the variant of the sonnet (to be discussed below) and a further examination of the context in which these techniques appear will both reveal that this apparent spontaneity belies a poem in which the choice of words and a strikingly idiosyncratic network of devices are executed with more than a modicum of care, control, and correction.

The most prominent technique to which Corbière gives his tacit sanction in the sonnet is verbal association. We have already examined some of the features of this device in "Litanie du sommeil"; let us now see how it relates to this sonnet's function as an *art poétique*. The sonnet manifests a thematic evolution resulting from the association of three words: "filés" in the first quatrain is succeeded by "télégraphe" in the second (immediately preceded, and announced by the root of "filés"), the prefix of which recurs in the "télégramme" which thematically dominates the tercets. Superficially, the constant motif of linearity—in the form of regularly fabricated verses, parallel wires, and messages sent from one point to another—shifts on the lexical level from thread (to rails, *en route*, in v. 5) to wires. The common denominator (the term is in keeping with the theme of mathematical monotony of Parnassian verse) of the "message" evolves from the poetic ("vers filés") to the banal ("raide"), elements which, in the poem's parodic context, are simply the two sides of a perfect equation.

But the technique of verbal association used by Corbière in this sonnet is far more complex than this and indeed demonstrates a conscious effort of organization on the part of the poet. There are five categories of linked expressions, each consisting of a series of words which are associated with others not only in the same stanza, but throughout the entire poem. Besides the "fils" (in regard to which the main thematic thread has been mentioned), they are *the military, sleep, classical allusions,* and *mathematics.* The process of "multiple linkage" alone suggests that Corbière is doing more than merely poking fun at a group of poets; to do this, he need not have gone to such elaborate lengths in the construction of the sonnet. He might well have, more simply, made direct use of Parnassian techniques or mentioned the poets under attack by name or made any number of extratextual allusions (all of which Rimbaud does, for instance, in his attack on the same group of poets, "Ce qu'on dit au poète à propos de fleurs"). What he has done instead is to interweave the five series, one giving constant way to another by verbal association, so that on a second, more important level of the poem (behind the parody), he is employing this apparently nonpoetic spontaneity as a conscious poetic device.

The first network of expressions begins with the second word of the sonnet—"filés." The threads sewn by the "faiseurs de vers" ("verse fabricators") are collected, in bunches of four, to form separate quatrains, in v. 2 ("en peloton"). The road to "le Pinde" (the mountain range of the Muses) is, ironically, by rail (a modern perversion of classical mythology), and *"railway"* and "ligne" continue the motif of mechanical (poetic) linearity begun by "filés." The rail soon becomes the "fils du télégraphe" (v. 6), by which, by transposition (the poetic context is established by "Pinde"), verses are figuratively transmitted. Corbière continues the parallel allusions to poetic and telegraphic communication in vv. 7–8, in which the two converge in a metaphor: the verses *are* telegraph wires, and each rhyme is a "pieu" (in the sense of *poteau,* "post") or a "jalon" (in the sense of *borne,* "marker"). The final expression in this group is the "raide" of v. 13: the tightening of Pegasus's reins by the "versificateur" ("professional versifier") completes the associations of stiffness and inflexibility present in the preceding allusions to wires and tracks. So, just as poetry is communicated stiffly from *pieu* to *pieu*, the poet's imaginative potential is stifled by the grounding of his patron quadruped.

In order to follow the second sequence of verbal associations (that of the military), we must now return to "filés" (v. 1), since, in a simile to follow, one of the four verses collected into a "peloton" is compared to "soldats de plomb." Any one of the verses, then, is a potential soldier (having been lulled to a stiff, standing sleep simply by the mechanical marking of the caesura, referred to in v. 3). This network of expressions (represented so far by "filés," "peloton," and "soldats de plomb") not only contains additional associations with the group already mentioned—expressed by two ambiguities: "filés" (verses which are sewn or soldiers in a line) and "peloton" (either a ball of thread or a platoon of soldiers)—but also announces yet a third group, to be examined presently, that of sleep (seen in both vv. 3 and 4). In retrospect, it is not only possible, but even clear that "uniforme" may be added to the list of words associated with the military motif. In the variant (the poem initially appeared in *La Cravache parisienne* on 19 May 1888, to be retained in the second [Vanier] edition of *Les Amours jaunes*, in 1891), the more explicit "en uniforme" appeared: the ellipsis of the preposition in the definitive version thus allows for both a literal interpretation and the more subtle expression of ambiguity. In fact, in the military context of the quatrain, "pied" and "pas" can be added to the group. The "raide" of v. 13 now has broader connotative value, since both wires and soldiers (as well as, of course, the verse under attack) are stiff; and the motifs, first joined in the opening quatrain, are again fused by this one adjective, at first glance functioning only as an epithet to describe the unfortunate "Pégase."

The allusions to sleep, inextricably tied to the military expressions of the first stanza (in addition to "s'endorme" and "dormir" is the probable play on words with *plomb* in v. 4: the "soldats de plomb" easily evokes the fixed expression, *sommeil de plomb*, "leaden sleep"), are also associated with the first group: the soldiers (verses) which may fall asleep in a vertical position announce the verticality of the telegraph pole ("pieu") of v. 7. The expressions of sleep, however, function primarily as analogues to the theme of linearity we have already seen in the movement of the soldiers and the various threads, lines, and wires of communication. "En long" (v. 6), referring to its antecedent, "fils (du télégraphe)," also announces the "pieu" of the subsequent verse. Both expressions illustrate a favorite device of Corbière's, the double-entendre: "en long," meaning "lengthwise," may also connote fatigue (as in the popular saying, *avoir les côtes en long*), while *pieu* is not only a post, but a bed as well. In v. 7, Corbière gives an ostensibly arbitrary example of rhyme—"*chloroforme*"—or at least it would so seem by the tone of the stanza and, indeed, of the entire poem. If we have been paying close attention, however, and are able to withdraw a moment from the parodic hilarity, we should see that the illustration offered by Corbière is not in the least arbitrary, but carefully chosen, its denotation consistent with the monotony—and now even soporific nature—of all the expressions heretofore examined (verses, lines of communication, soldiers, sleep).

The category of classical allusions is altogether fitting for this particular parody. Themes and allusions in so many Parnassian poems were, we recall, of classical antiquity (in addition to the very name of this "movement"), as, for instance, in the *vers d'antiquité* of poets like Leconte de Lisle, Ménard, and Banville. The "Pinde" of v. 5 is followed, in turn, by the "Muse d'Archimède" which Tristan mischievously invokes (v. 10), "Pégase" (v. 13), and the classical "lyre" (v. 14). As with "uniforme," "pied," in retrospect, gains additional meaning: the parodied verse, associated with the Greek poetry it extolled, can now be perceived as being written in "feet" ("pied") and not, as is traditional in France, in syllables. Is Corbière not intimating here that his new, liberated verse, so different from that of his "classical" contemporaries, is in reality more "French" than theirs? If we accept that he wrote this sonnet (and, indeed, if it is to be viewed as a kind of *ars poetica*, then so many other poems) with more care and "art" than its ostensibly off-handed manner would suggest, then it is perhaps not a farfetched hypothesis that, having had a certain training in the French poetic tradition, he might have had Boileau's "Art poétique" (1674) in mind as a tangential target. In the latter's lengthy text, do not the expressions "Parnasse" and "Pégase est rétif" appear in the very first stanza? (They thus correspond, in Corbière's poem, first to both the neoclassical nature and name of the nineteenth-century poetic group parodied, and second to the final *hémistiche* of v. 13.)

The final category of associated words—related, as are the previous ones, to the monotony of the parodied verse—is composed of mathematical expressions and allusions. Sonnenfeld calls the Parnassian method which the sonnet mocks a "problème de calcul," a "leçon de calligraphie et d'arithmétique." Superficially, this is what the sonnet does berate, but the use of mathematical terms in the poem itself constitutes at the same time a conscious transgression of a poetic proscription: Corbière uses actual *chiffres* ("numerals") in vv.9, 12, and 13. Furthermore, the equal sign of v. 12 is not only absent from the syllable-count (and is thus the most outrageous kind of "padding" imaginable), but it also nullifies the silent *e* of the "quatre" which precedes it—an *e* which, in standard prosody, is itself unacceptable (the placement of a mute *e* immediately before the caesura). Finally, the substitution of the Roman numeral for the indefinite article in the title is, from a traditional standpoint, equally deplorable. Thus, if the parody is directed, in part, against the mechanical, "mathematical" Parnassian verse, Corbière uses the very tools of his critical target as his own poetic devices. Completing this group of verbal associations are "quatre" (vv. 2, 3, and 6), "la ligne" (v. 5), "Archimède" (v. 10), and "par addition" (v. 11).

In order to evaluate fully Corbière's use of verbal association in "I Sonnet," we might take a collective look at the five categories.

| category | verse numbers |
|---|---|
| "fils," etc. | 1, 2, 5, 5, 5, 6, 7, 8, 8, 13 |
| military | 1, 2, 4, 13, 14 |
| sleep | 3, 4, 6, 7, 7 |
| classical allusions | 5, 10, 13, 14, subscription |
| mathematics | title, 2, 3, 5, 6, 9, 10, 11, 12, 13 |

The expressions are interwoven in such a manner that, of the fourteen verses, only four (8, 9, 11, 12) do not manifest a coexistence of categories. What makes this statistic significant is that all five categories are clearly interrelated: verbal and mechanical communication, military discipline, sleep, classicism, and mathematics are in some way symptomatic of the poetry under attack. The associations in the poem are not "automatic"—neither the free associations of, for instance, the "aviary" section of Apollinaire's "Zone" nor the celebrated "pure psychic automatism" of which Breton speaks in his *Manifeste du surréalisme* of 1924. They are, rather, by their compactness and bi-directional nature, controlled ones, and rather typical in regard to Corbière's poetic output. A final piece of evidence to this claim: expressions which do *not* appear in the variant, but *do* in the definitive version—"filés," "s'endorme," "fils du télégraphe," "railway du Pinde," "en long," and "pieu"—represent alterations which indicate Corbière's unquestionably aesthetic motivation. Furthermore, is it by pure chance that, with the exception of vv. 9 and 12, every end-rhyme in the sonnet represents a "key" word—often (vv. 1, 2, 4, 6, 13) with multiple connotations? This procedure of "linked rhymes" is surely a recognizable trait of Corbière's, as we have seen in "Litanie du sommeil."

Verbal associations are only one, albeit the most striking of the typically Corbiérian stylistic devices used in "I Sonnet." Another, appearing so frequently throughout his poetry, is the *jeu de mots*, consisting of puns, incongruities, and double-entendres. It seems that these poetic devices appear in a particularly frequent and compact form in this sonnet; this is especially meaningful in a poem the motive of which *appears* to be the criticism of other poets, and not the formulation of a creative method by the "critic" himself.

The pun appears (besides the "plomb" of v. 4) four times in "I Sonnet." In the initial verse, Corbière juxtaposes the opposites "main/pied," not only creating an obviously caustic effect at the expense of the Parnassian handcrafters, but also, in terms of the "pied" part, announcing the subsequent classical allusions and the "pas" of v. 2. This pun was not present in the variant (the original opening verse read, "Je vais faire un sonnet; des vers en uniforme," "I'll make a sonnet; verses in uniform"), again demonstrating the effort Corbière made to refine the text. He also plays on the etymology of "délire" (v. 14): seeming to mock the Romantic poets in the final verse (their overflowing the boundaries of classical propriety is paralleled by his purposefully exorbitant use of assonance), he "de-lyres" ("dé/lyre") the instrument *they* use as well. Although Corbière himself states "J'ai lavé ma lyre" ("I've hocked my lyre") in v. 5 of "Ça?," the presumption consistent with the thesis of the present analysis is that this lyre is the classical one and that Corbière had no intention of giving up the writing of poetry, as, of course, was borne out by his subsequent poetic activity. Indeed, the lyres of both Parnassian and Romantic alike are stripped of their strings, but Tristan's "crincrin" (the expression is Laforgue's) is the only survivor in this sonnet, and very much alive at that. Another "etymologism," "uniforme" (v. 1), can, from its Latin roots, mean "equal" (ameliorative sense) or, in the context of what follows, "monotonous" (pejorative). This play on words is immediately followed by yet another: "Emboîtant" (v. 2), modifying "vers," literally denotes *suivre*, "to follow" (used with "pas"); but, following "pied," it also suggests the verb *boîter*, which perverts the "step" of the verse from a steady one to a limp.

The use of juxtaposed incongruous expressions is common in Corbière's poems and appears three times in this one. The *"railway du Pinde"* (v. 5) is an anachronistic juxtaposition which serves to devalue the classical allusion, just as a second expression, "d'Archimède," undercuts the "Muse" it modifies (v. 10). In the latter use of incongruity—technically, an oxymoron—it is now the subject, and not the possessive, which is the victim of this device. A third expression, "télégramme sacré" (v. 9), utters the adjective in vain (*sacré* means "blasted" or "cursed" in its popular sense) by allying it to a mechanism which is utilitarian in nature. Again, what Corbière succeeds in doing in these three examples is not only to desecrate the sacred Parnassian Muse, but also to consecrate his own.

The double- (or, in some cases, triple-) entendre is the most frequent of these *jeux de mots*. Besides those already discussed (the two meanings of "pied," "pieu," and "en long" and the three of *"ligne"*—poetic, telegraphic, and mathematical), Corbière employs another: "filés" (v. 1). In addition to the two possibilities of this word mentioned above ("sewn verses," a line of soldiers), the adjective can also mean "developed," as in "métaphore filée."

Still another area of revolt prescribed by Corbière in "I Sonnet" resides in the poem's syntax and phrasing. Regarding the disposition of the caesura and the syllable-count, the sonnet is (with the exception of the suppressed silent *e* of "quatre" in v. 12) nearly classical. Corbière's use of ellipsis and unorthodox punctuation, however, undermines the poem's conventional versification and gives further evidence of an apparently spontaneous method. Ellipsis of the verb occurs in vv. 7, 8, and 12 (and, in the final verse, something on the order of "C'est un" is omitted between syllables 6 and 7); and the suppression of the article is apparent in vv. 4, 7, and 9.[12] The sonnet's unorthodox punctuation is another aspect of Corbière's prosody very much in evidence, and which proves to be strongly idiosyncratic during the course of his volume. In fact, more than any other technique, it illustrates how this sonnet functions as an *ars poetica* while appearing to be just the contrary. In the process of belittling "Le Parnasse" for its "telegraphic" verse, Corbière makes literal use of it, giving a brilliant demonstration on his own terms, with the end result a contemptuous deconstruction of conventional poetic diction. Statistically, the poem contains three ellipses, three colons, one parenthesis, six exclamation points, and thirteen dashes. It is, however, their placement that demonstrates Corbière's artifice, reflecting the desired evolution from *af*fective to *de*fective punctuation. The pace begins slowly, with the ellipsis in v. 3 (pausing for a nap) as the only "defect" in an otherwise smooth-flowing stanza. Although an increase in punctuation in the second quatrain adds a conversational tone not present in the initial stanza, the rhythmic equilibrium is still maintained, as the pauses represented by dash and colon are strategically (and obediently) placed at the beginning of a verse, at the caesura, or at the *coupe* following the ninth syllable (v. 7). But the use of these signs as an affective technique quickly gives way to a seemingly gratuitous accumulation of punctuation, used not to express, but rather to dislocate the message. On the one hand, the poet/persona desperately attempts to control his expression within the sonnet's confines (vv. 10, 13, 14); but Corbière, on the other, has destroyed the sonnet's rhythmic integrity: the mechanism has broken down, as disjunctive pauses now come successively (and rebelliously), now after the eighth syllable (v. 9), now after the second (v. 10), seventh (v. 12), second again, fifth, and eighth (all in v. 14), until the final verse concludes the poem in a paroxysm of rhythmic and semantic chaos.

The results of the preceding analysis suggest a conclusion that Corbière's poetic method is a conscious one and that his techniques are not haphazard but, rather, decidedly purposeful. What should be most evident is that it is inadvisable to take the mischievous Tristan at his word. The lesson of "Ça?" is not a literal one: "Ça?" is still poetry, and if Corbière has traded in his lyre, it is only because its classical harmony was inimical to his very personal method of performance. Claiming that his poetry results from *raccroc* or *hasard*, he has shown us, at least in "I Sonnet," that this claim was so much lip-service and just another pose. For even in a poem of such seeming transparency, Corbière is at his deceptive best. Behind the Dionysian and irreverent dismantling of the Parnassian prosodic method, Tristan/Apollo has created his own: the synthesis of verbal associations, puns, etymologisms, incongruities, double-

entendres, *chiffres*, borrowings, linked rhymes, ellipsis, and aberrant punctuation produces a display of virtuosity which stands by
itself, beyond the primary level of parody so immediately accessible
to the reader. Seemingly offhanded and unpolished, his verse—not
only in "I Sonnet," but throughout— is, paradoxically, carefully
cultivated, a judgment with which Michel Dansel so eloquently
agrees:

> this absence of affection, this lack of polishing are willed, even sought
> after, and are created by a patient application of the work on the [poetic]
> craft, even though the author makes himself out to be a stumbling amateur.[13]

Cradled lovingly, Corbière's *violon* was muted (in "I Sonnet"
behind a foreground of parody, elsewhere by strains of claimed
inefficacy),—and perceptibly scratchy—but there nonetheless,
making a new and strange kind of music, despite its owner's insistence to the contrary.

### IV    *The Un-tempered Clavier, or "Shoot the Piano-Tuner"*

A never-anthologized little poem which has also successfully
managed to escape critical scrutiny is "À une demoiselle. Pour piano
et chant." It is rather similar to "I Sonnet" in regard to the indirect
manner by which it posits its own aesthetics; whereas the latter
poem does this at the expense of a poetic technique which it attacks,
the aesthetic target of "À une demoiselle" is a false way of emoting
and of self-expression. Why aesthetic? Because the damsel who is
criticized is described metaphorically as a piano, and because the
means of expression contrasted with this artificial one is in fact
Corbière's poetry ("cet accord de ma lyre," v. 9), what is under
attack is not only the feelings themselves, but also the agent of this
expression—in particular, a specific type of music (and, by extension, of poetry):

La dent de ton Érard, râtelier osanore,
Et scie et broie à cru, sous son tic-tac nerveux,
La gamme de tes dents, autre clavier sonore. . .
Touches qui ne vont pas aux cordes des cheveux!

—Cauchemar de meunier, ta: *Rêverie agile!*
—Grattage, ton: *Premier amour à quatre mains!*
Ô femme transposée en *Morceau difficile,*
Tes croches sans douleur n'ont pas d'accents humains!

Déchiffre au clavecin cet accord de ma lyre;
Télégraphe à musique, il pourra le traduire:
Cris d' os, dur, sec, qui plaque et casse—Plangorer. . .

Jamais!—La *clef-de-Sol* n'est pas la clef de l'âme,
La *clef-de-Fa* n'est pas la syllabe de *Femme,*
Et deux *demi-soupirs* . . .ce n' est pas soupirer.

The tooth of your Érard, falsified denture,
Saws and crunches its tired old nervous air,
The scale of your teeth, another musical adventure . . .
Keys which don't go to the strings of your hair!
—A miller's nightmare, your: *Agile Reveries!*
—Scratchings, your: *First Love for Four Hands!*
O woman turned into a *Difficult Piece,*
Your sorrow-less eighth-notes have no human strands!

Decipher on your harpsichord this tune from my lyre;
Musical telegraph, become versifier:
Bone-shrieks, hard and dry, which strike and break—Moan and cry . . .

Never!—*G* isn't the soul's key,
Nor is *F* the syllable of *Effeminacy,*
And two *eighth-rests* . . .don't mean repose and sigh.

Once again, Corbière attempts to throw us off our guard from the very outset. The unassuming title and evocative subtitle set the scene of love and music to follow, suggesting tenderness and lyricism appropriately accompanied by a musical background. This is short-lived, however, despite the opening words ("La dent de ton . . . "), which seem to be announcing some kind of *blason* in honor of the damsel of the title. Just as in Rimbaud's "Le Cœur volé," where the melancholic opening hemistich ("Mon triste cœur," "My sad heart") is brutally undermined by the second ("bave à la poupe," "dribbles on the poop"), here an ironic "note" intrudes: the poet is speaking not of his lady's tooth, but of the "fake" keys of her piano, which plays nothing but artificial notes. From this point on, both the lady and her instrument are under constant attack; and, as we shall discover, the title and subtitle accrue an irony not immediately apparent to us.

Before we examine how Corbière indirectly states his aesthetic, we should briefly summarize what is going on in this poem, which is perhaps more difficult than the usual Corbière offering. In the first stanza, Corbière deftly presents us with a pair of "reciprocal" metaphors: not only is the lady's piano described as dentures, but her teeth are transformed into a(nother) "clavier sonore," "sonorous keyboard." Next, the tunes played by both transformed metaphors (but particularly the lady herself, who has become a *"Morceau difficile"*) are described as scratchings, lacking the human touch. The damsel has become an automaton, playing (and thus emoting) the same monotonous song. The tone shifts in the tercets to pleading, and although there are interpretative difficulties in the first tercet, a contrast between Corbière's lyre and the lady's harpsichord is clearly established. He asks her to decipher, or translate, on *her* instrument (i.e., metaphorically, in her own emotive way), described as a monotonous "musical telegraph," *this* harmony of *his* lyre. Since there is no antecedent for the demonstrative ("cet"), the meaning arises from the context: "cet accord" refers, and is in apposition, to what follows the colon in v.10, i.e.,"Cris d'os, dur, sec, qui plaque et casse." Since "Déchiffre" and "traduire" are parallel expressions, the pronoun "il" refers to "clavecin" (and its appositive, "télégraphe"), and the direct object "le" corresponds to "cet accord," to be "translated." A curious ellipsis follows, at the conclusion of v. 11. One means of "translating" the "accord" would be "Plangorer," a neologism meaning "to bemoan." As in "I Sonnet," this "Romantic" solution is rejected ("Jamais!"). In the final tercet, Corbière explains that neither type of music offered by the lady (plaintive, monotonous) is adequate to express what is in the "soul," what is the essence of Woman, what is love. The entire poem, on a second reading, is, then, metaphorical: Tristan is speaking not of bridgework and keyboards, but of means of expression; and it is significant that the rejected means, as in "I Sonnet," but even more obliquely, correspond precisely to two known methods of *poetic* expression: Romantic and Parnassian. The key to poetry is to express the essence of things (the soul, love, etc.); this cannot be accomplished by standard musical (poetic) means, but by those unorthodox techniques utilized by Corbière himself.

Once again, the essential statement of the "correct" manner of self-expression appears not directly (although v. 11 is rather explicit). but in Corbière's poetic performance. The fundamental aspects of the lady's expression (and music) which pervert her quest for the Truth are *monotony* ("et scie et broie à cru," "tic-tac nerveux," "cauchemar de meunier," "télégraphe à musique"), *artifice* ("râtelier osanore"; the "keys" which do not correspond to the "strings" elsewhere [i.e., teeth and hair lack a sensual unity in the lady]; the "practiced" musical pieces she plays in stanza 2; and the inadequate "logic" of musical notation in the final tercet), and *lyricism or harmony* (the subtitle; the ironic "sonore," a possible oblique attack on Hugo's "écho sonore"; and "Plangorer"). Against these elements, Corbière proffers his own, which all attempt to capture the quintessence of affective experience: *variety, spontaneity,* and *discord.*

Again, as in "I Sonnet," what appears to be simply an attack is, more subtly, a defense of methodology. The variety lacking in the monotones of the lady/piano manifests itself rhythmically in the poet/lyre, particularly in the manipulation of caesurae. Verses 1–4, 7–10, and 14 are essentially "classical," equally divided into two hemistiches by a median caesura. By contrast, vv. 5–6 and 11–13 are uneven (with caesurae after the second, fourth, seventh, and ninth syllables) or choppy (broken up by colon, dash, and comma). By breaking through the traditional bounds of the sonnet, Corbière can more truly reflect the conflicts and hesitations in his soul.

If the mathematical precision and limitations of music (poetry) inhibit its ability to communicate freely and completely, then the spontaneity of the sonnet itself removes these barriers and allows Corbière to reach his goal (of "being himself"). Punctuation appears—as it does so often—unexpectedly, as ellipses (3), exclamation points (5), dashes (4), and colons (3) intrude whenever they are called upon to express Corbière's thought at the moment (e.g., the excessive punctuation in vv. 11–12, expressing our poet's internal monologue). The play on words, reflecting the "essential" Tristan, also abounds, eminently representing the "accent humain" resonating from his lyre and absent in the automated scratchings of his lady's piano. First, what is a "dent de piano" ("piano tooth")? Apparently nothing, according to the best dictionaries. "Dent de scie" ("serration," "saw's tooth") does exist, however; what Corbière has done is to manufacture the expression "dent de piano" (this is close to being a neologism, another means by which he innovates with seeming spontaneity: in fact, there is an example of this technique in v. 11—"Plangorer," from the Latin *plangere,* "to bewail") and then justify the new usage by the subsequent verb, "scier," "To bore or fatigue." This is the verb's familiar meaning; its literal meaning, "to saw," imparts to the word "dent" the double possibility of being a saw's tooth moving monotonously back and forth ("scie et broie à cru"), or a real tooth (indeed, "Érard"—a brand of piano—is transformed into a set of dentures by metaphor) crunching ("broie") in a regular rhythm. In transforming the lady into a piano, into a "difficult piece," Corbière also alters the "first piece for four hands" to "first love for four hands," thus contaminating the musical allusion with a "romantic" notion. The same kind of contamination occurs in the previous verse, where the "Agile reverie" is in apposition to the "miller's nightmare," or the monotony of the grinding of the mill. Words are also happily manipulated (what could be less artificial to Corbière?) in each of the final three verses of the sonnet.

Let us proceed backwards in order to justify the claim of trickery in v. 12. In music, two eighth-rests do, of course, make a quarter-rest (two "demi-soupirs" equal one "soupir"). But the expected "soupir" is replaced by the verb "soupirer" (the lover's sigh), and the equation of musical notation and affective experience cannot be tolerated. Likewise, the key of "F" cannot embody Womanhood: the resemblance in sound—[fa]—is purely coincidental. It is only natural that the twelfth verse join in the fun, . . . but how? Since there are no semantic or phonetic links between "Sol" and "âme," the only possibility is the English homonym for "Sol," "soul," which also happens to be the translation for . . . "âme"! If this sounds incredible, we can turn to other precedents, such as the "Attention" in "I Sonnet" (which might suggest the English military exclamation, in the context of that poem) and, closer to home, v. 11 of this poem. If "Sol" and "âme" were chosen with such loving care (which we must, for the moment, assume), then perhaps "Cris d'os," a rather strange conjoining of words, may have been conceived with another play on words in mind: can it not refer to the English homonym, "Credo"? After all, "cet accord de ma lyre" (the *Cris d'os*) was one of the few entities in which Corbière had any *belief*.

There are even more subtle possibilities for word-games (if we cannot be certain—can we ever be with Corbière?—at least we can give Tristan the benefit of the doubt, for in many ways he was a poet of extreme subtlety) in the poem's title and subtitle, which suggest that here, as so often elsewhere in his verse, Corbière was more interested in "ludic" than in "lyric" poetry. After we have seen the lady metamorphosed into a piano, we can now substitute her for the "piano" of the subtitle, which leaves a rather ridiculous redundancy in the double dedication (consistent with the motif of "monotony"): "À une demoiselle. Pour demoiselle. . . ." We may even wonder why he is dedicating the poem to her in the first place; in fact, if we look at Corbière's poetry carefully, we find well-documented precedence for his referring to his Muse as a "demoiselle" ("Muse pucelle" in "Paris [*Bâtard de Créole et Breton*]," "fille/D'amour, d'oisiveté, de prostitution" in "Décourageux," as well as in "Libertà" and several other poems). Indeed, Corbière looked upon his Muse as a kind of *courtisane*, with no attachments (least of all to him) and no possessive preoccupations. With this in mind, we can now reconsider the title, not as a song dedicated to his fair lady (he had none, save the unrequiting Marcelle, and the "demoiselle" is significantly preceded by an indefinite article, not a possessive adjective), but to the only woman who asked (and was given) nothing in return, his Muse. In this light, the metaphoric value of the sonnet is further corroborated: the *real* subject is poetry, his own in particular, and if the poem is dedicated *for* Tristan's Muse, the irony might also be extended to the subtitle, where "Contre" may be substituted for "Pour" with impunity.

After the substitution of spontaneity for artifice, Corbière's replacement of discord for harmony is most apparent in the way in which he structures the poem. Once again reminiscent of "I Sonnet" (but not of the third month), the poem comes in like a lamb and goes out like a lion. The quatrains are almost entirely composed of nearly classical alexandrines, structured in a parallel manner: in each case, the first three verses present a series of separate negative statements, resolved—the term is to be construed in its musical sense as well—in the stanza's final verse, which extracts the essence of the preceding verses (in both cases, the "inhuman" aspects of the lady's playing). Once Corbière begins to wander to thoughts of his *own* poetry, however, the balance is destroyed, its harmony replaced by the chaos and discord of the tercets. Two of the explicitly stated qualities of his poetry—"qui plaque et casse"—are implicit in his practice. First, the final three verses are neither "resolved" harmoniously nor are they "scratchings": Corbière bangs out his message loud and clear ("dur," "sec"). More importantly, the tercets break or dislocate what has preceded. What was balance is now chaos, seen in the unpredictability of punctuation, rhythm, and even syntax: vv. 9–10 must be read with more care, and the ellipsis in vv. 11–12 interrupts the dialogue between the poet and his damsel simply by eliminating the latter and turning the poet's thoughts inward. The key phrase in the poem is surely "cet accord de ma lyre." The irony implicit in it is that what is traditionally seen as "harmony" is rejected by Corbière in his pejorative treatment of expressions which connote this very quality: *piano, gamme, clavier, touches, cordes, croches, clavecin, musique, clef.* In contrast, true harmony, only possible from *his* poetic instrument, resides in what is traditionally seen as discordant ("Cris d'os, dur, sec, qui plaque et casse"); for Tristan, there is at least nothing phony or learned or mechanical about these sounds which he creates.

This conflict between Corbière's discord and traditional lyricism is yet another in a series of differences which we have seen between our poet and his contemporaries. The abyss separating his perspective and that of his peers is apparent in the expressions "Déchiffre" and "il pourra le traduire": the verb "pourra," an implied conditional, is wishful thinking on the part of the harpsichord, which will never be in tune with the Corbiérian lyre. For so many poets of nineteenth-century France, music and the approximation of poetry to song was of capital importance. Allusions to Pan, Orpheus, and the (classical) Muse and lyre abound, and the primacy of the Song in poetry (in euphony, structure, and versification) is recognized, from the early Romantics to end-of-the-century poets like Paul Fort and Henri de Régnier. We think of Musset's *luth* and Rimbaud's *violon* and *clairon* (in his letters to Izambard and Demeny); of theoretical speculations of, among others, Hugo, Baudelaire, Verlaine, Banville, and René Ghil; and of the influence on French poets of not only French music (e.g., Berlioz, Debussy), but also of Spanish serenades and the German *lieder* and Wagner. But for Corbière, the adherence to traditional rules and concepts of harmony or lyricism resulted inexorably in an intolerable lie perpetrated by the musician, the Poet, or, in "À une demoiselle," the lady.

## CHAPTER 4

# Far from the Madding Crowd

## I  Tristan and Sisyphus

AT the risk of isolating *forme* (style) from *fond* (content), we should now consider the major motifs of Corbière's poetry. In point of fact, the "risk" will not be taken, since the same type of detailed analyses of our poet's style which preceded will be an integral part of the discussion of his essential subjects (exile, heterosexual love, Brittany, death) which will fill the remaining chapters of this volume.

A text which might ease the transition from Corbière's manner of writing to the motif of exile (or isolation) is Albert Camus's *Le Mythe de Sisyphe*.[1] Two of the major sections of this essay—entitled "L'Homme absurde" and "La Création absurde"—reflect rather well Tristan's situation as writer and as human being. In regard to "absurd creativity," Camus writes:

In this regard, the perfect absurd joy is creating. "Art and nothing but art, said Nietzsche, we have art in order not to die from the truth." . . . In this world, the work is thus the only chance to maintain one's conscience and to fix one's adventures. To create is to live twice. . . . Everyone tries to mimic, to repeat and to recreate the reality which is his own. We always end up by wearing the face of our truths. The whole of existence for a man obstructed from the Eternal is but a boundless imitation under the mask of the absurd. Creating is the ultimate imitation.

Tristan, himself "obstructed from the Eternal," certainly fits this description of the "absurd man" who attempts to affirm himself, to create (or "recreate"), in some unique way (in this case, poetic), his own identity. But let us now proceed to one of the essential sources of this poetic creativity of Corbière's—a profound feeling of exile, of separation from the rest of humanity—once again, by way of an earlier passage from Camus's essay which defines the absurd existence:

What is then this incalculable feeling which deprives the mind of the sleep essential to its life? A world which one can explain even with faulty reasoning is a familiar world. But on the contrary, in a universe suddenly deprived of illusions and enlightenment, man feels himself a stranger. This exile is irreversible since it is without memories of a lost homeland or of the hope of a promised land. This divorce between man and his life, the actor and his décor, is precisely the feeling of absurdity. All healthy men having contemplated their own suicide, one can recognize, without further explanation, that there is a direct rapport between this feeling and the aspiration toward the void.

There is, in this passage, an eerie reflection of Corbière, seventy years after the fact. In addition to the elements of insomnia, figurative loss of sight, and a desire to plunge into the void, the expressions marked by prefixes of excision and estrangement ("étranger," "exil," "divorce") accurately characterize Tristan's "absurd" existence. There are, however, major differences between Camus's absurd man and Corbière's condition. First, the contemplation of suicide resulting from the absurd life is a normative phenomenon, whereas Corbière's plight, as we shall see, has no trace of collectivity. Second, whereas the refusal of suicide allows Camus's absurd man to pursue the triple ideals of revolt, freedom, and passion, Corbière, like Hamlet or, better, Gide's Michel (in *L'Immoraliste*), is not only isolated but seems to be unable to pursue specific goals, attain specific direction, or discover active solutions to this isolation. Finally, the epigraph of Camus's essay (like that of Valéry's "Le Cimetière marin") is taken from Pindar's third *Pythic:* "O my soul, do not aspire to eternal life, but exhaust what is possible." In Corbière's case, this ideal of plenitude is perverted: the poet's self-perception is almost always one of failure, not heroism.

## II   *Exile*

The topos of exile is of course a familiar one in the context of French (and world) literature, yet Corbière's treatment of it is (as was everything else he did) rather unorthodox. There is neither need nor space to trace the theme of exile and isolation from its beginnings in French literature. For our purposes, it will suffice to say that the varieties of exile in the collective poetic experience are great, ranging from logistical estrangement (from, say, Du Bellay's *Les Regrets* to expatriate verse like Supervielle's) to politically imposed exile (of which Voltaire and Hugo are perhaps the most illustrious instances) to what we might call "imaginative exile." The latter psychic phenomenon, by which the poet transported himself away from the mediocrity or melancholy of the *ici-bas* to some sort of metaphysical or spiritual shelter, was most prevalent in early nineteenth-century literature and stands in striking contrast to Corbière's handling of the same problem. In the case of the Romantic conception of spiritual exile, the basis of the divorce from everyday existence was the pride and feeling of superiority of the poet and his heightened sensitivity. Hence, Keats's bower, Vigny's tower, Stendhal's "happy few," Lamartine's "isolation," and, more generally, the tremendous attraction during these years toward exoticism and reverie.

In contrast, the subversive element of Corbière's self-exile resides in his concept of Self and of his place within the context of humanity as a whole. Perhaps his closest "modern" *confrère* is the contemporary poet-singer Georges Brassens, who, like Corbière, did his share of nose-thumbing. Their common bonds are the conception of the Self as an outsider and an identification with the oppressed and downtrodden individual, for whom they felt an instinctive empathy. With Brassens's *brav's gens*, or the "upstanding gentry" (in "La mauvaise réputation"), for example, the playful irony recalls the righteous bourgeoisie of Charles Cros:

> But the good folk say "Beware!"
> If you follow a different road from theirs,
> Everybody smears my name,
> Except the mutes, they're not to blame.

In stanzas 2–4 of this poem-song, other fraternal "sympathizers" (or at least nonchastizers) are substituted for the mutes: "the one-armed," "the legless," "the blind": cf., significantly, Corbière's "Cris d'aveugle."

What separates Corbière's exile from all of the above is his conception of his own "nonselfhood." The Romantic isolation was a noble one, based on an exalted view of the Self. In the cases of Voltaire and Hugo, exile was politically motivated and, in fact, was not only the genesis of creative stimulation (at Ferney and the

Channel Islands, respectively), but also resulted in adulation on their return to *la patrie*. For Corbière, there was no question of nobility or martyrdom. Exile and isolation were not simply from the mediocrity of the *vulgus* or the security of the homeland: they were, in fact, from the human race as a whole. Exile was neither intellectual motivation nor simple literary motif, but rather a constant, profound, and obsessive element of his (non-)human condition. This conception of Self as subhuman, often ironically stated but nonetheless poignantly adhered to, is best expressed in "Le Poète contumace," in which Tristan describes himself (as poet-persona) as "En dehors de l'humaine piste" ("Outside the human race"). His misanthropy is thus perfectly objective (not being *anthropos* himself); he is an anchorite without an anchor.

What follows from this is that rather than identify himself with higher forms of life or idealized humans (we can compare, for instance, the rare intelligence and sensitivity of most Romantic heroes, or the parallels with and solicitations of a whole host of biblical and mythological figures), Corbière presents himself either as beast (e.g., a lost dog in "Elizir d'amor" and a toad in "Le Crapaud") or as some human aberrant, rejected by and exiled from humanity, mostly for physical reasons (the empirical source, from Tristan's own life, is self-evident): beggars, prisoners, deaf, blind, and one-eyed people, the lame and the hunchbacked (in contrast, once again, to Camus's "healthy men").

It is often difficult to separate Corbière's desire for self-knowledge from his penchant for self-flagellation. We can, however, characterize the isolation itself in regard to its various manifestations: exile from family, from home (even from his beloved Breton countryside, in "Le Poète contumace"), from Self, from humanity, from normal communication (hence his stylistic idiosyncrasies), and, finally, from life itself (from which results, as we shall discuss later in chapter 5, a preoccupation with the death motif). Consequently, what strikes the reader in Corbière's verse is this permanent demarcation between a faceless abstraction of a world at large and a homeless, exiled, even solipsistic figure of a poet.

### III   *The Swan and the Cuckoo*

Before discussing what are perhaps Corbière's most outstanding poems of isolation—"Le Poète contumace" and "Rapsodie du sourd"—we might first contrast his "Paria" to Baudelaire's "Le

Cygne" in order to understand better his personal brand of exile and of poetic expression of this theme. Of all the swans in the French lyric tradition, Baudelaire's—along with Mallarmé's in *"Le vierge, le vivace et le bel aujourd'hui. . ."*—is probably the most illustrious. Also like the Mallarmé text, but even more so, Baudelaire's "Le Cygne" is a poem of exile, of estrangement and incongruity, one of the most startlingly evocative examples ever written.

Briefly (thus, superficially), "Le Cygne" is a two-part narrative which consists of a series of reflections which pass through the poet's mind during a Paris walk. In Part I, the artificial river built by the exiled Andromache, the "false Simoïs" (reminding her of her native Troy), seems to have jogged Baudelaire's memory (as he crosses the "New Carrousel") of a former visual image of Paris, in which his mind's eye recalls having seen a swan who had somehow escaped from its cage and was pitifully dragging its feathers on the unfamiliar dusty pavement:

> Un cygne qui s'était évadé de sa cage,
> Et, de ses pieds palmés frottant le pavé sec,
> Sur le sol raboteux traînait son blanc plumage.
> Près d'un ruisseau sans eau la bête ouvrant le bec
>
> Baignait nerveusement ses ailes dans la poudre,
> Et disait, le cœur plein de son beau lac natal:
> "Eau, quand donc pleuvras-tu? quand tonneras-tu, foudre?"
>
> A swan who had escaped from its cage,
> And, rubbing the dry pavement with its webbed feet,
> On the rugged ground dragged its white plumage.
> Near a dried-up stream the beast, opening its beak,
>
> Nervously bathed its wings in the dusty gloom,
> And said, its heart filled with its fine native lake:
> "Water, when will you pour? thunder, when will you boom?"

In Part II, the chronology is altered to reconstitute for us the *real* sequence of events. Andromache, who opens the poem, gives way to Paris and then to the swan. Now, a changing Paris becomes an allegorical statement of exile, evoking first swan, then Andromache, and finally, in the last three stanzas, a proliferation of exiled personages, from the consumptive Negress searching for the lost coconut groves of her native Africa behind a wall of Parisian fog to a collective mass of lost sailors, prisoners, . . . and still others ("bien d'autres encor!").

It is indeed a pity to have to truncate this magnificent text for the purposes of this contrastive study. In any event, the two basic strategies of the Baudelaire poem are the universalization of the swan and the consequent affective dramatization of the exile experience. In the first case, the central figure of the swan is not only anthropomorphized—introduced simply as an animal ("la bête"), it soon exhibits the abilities to emote ("le cœur plein de son beau lac natal", "ce malheureux"), to speak, and to cerebrate ("Comme s'il adressait des reproches à Dieu," "as if reproaching God [for his condition]")—but the juxtaposition of the title with the opening word of the poem ("Andromaque") gives to it a classical nobility later confirmed by Baudelaire's subsequent allusions: "mythe étrange et fatal" ("strange and fatal myth") and "mon grand cygne," who, like Baudelaire's albatross of a different poem, is "ridicule et sublime." In regard to the exile topos, this is indeed the entire "symbolic" point of the poem. All the examples propagated by the poet's imagination are characterized by incongruity and estrangement, thus evoking the pity and compassion of the reader. Reaffirming this aspect are both the heightened drama of Part II, created by a noticeable rhythmic acceleration and a proliferation of exclamation points; and the dedication of the poem, "À Victor Hugo," which, placed between the swan (of the title) and Andromache, links the two from the outset in regard to their status as *exilés*, since, at the time, Hugo (then in Guernesey) was the living symbol of this phenomenon.

It is literally needless to say (nevertheless, . . . ) that Baudelaire's verse (conception, style, etc.) differed greatly from Tristan's. The contrast is particularly significant regarding "Le Cygne" and "Paria." Baudelaire's title is a universal one, Corbière's nondescript. "Le Cygne" is a calculated, self-conscious text, complete with premeditated structure, dramatic development, and central focus, whereas "Paria" is an amorphous series of emissions. The incongruity of the swan and its analogues is dramatized to produce a maximum effect of pathos, while Tristan's situation of incongruity in an alien world could not be more natural to the poet and is stated with a certain nonchalance. The noble (and figurative) universalizing of "inner feelings" by analogy (the swan, Andromache, etc.) contrasts with the solitary (*and literal*) figure of the ignoble Tristan.

Finally, the choice of the swan, a traditional symbol of beauty and purity and a frequent metaphor for the poet, could not be further from that of Corbière's cuckoo, the homeless maverick and perpetual home-moocher. From the point of view of evocative power and formal beauty, there is no doubt at all of the superiority of Baudelaire's poem. But Corbière's game was not this sort of evocation or conscious structuring and organizing (as was Baudelaire's, or Hugo's, for that matter), but rather (again, this familiar leitmotif) the presentation of Self—in this case, an exiled Self—by means of a very personal use of word choice and word-play, which an examination of key stanzas of "Paria" (a typically rambling poem of thirteen stanzas) will now attempt to demonstrate.[2]

Stanzas 1–5 and 8–9 all attempt to present the various *absences* in the absurd life of the outcast Tristan, the absence of which would offer him some grounding in, or commitment to, "real" life as we know it: politics and domesticity, sensibility, domicile, love, dreams, poetry (or poetic thought and voice), and temporal orientation, respectively. As in all good poetry, however, it is not simply this theme and its variations that should interest the reader, but the manner in which they are presented. The two outstanding (and familiar) Corbiérian idiosyncrasies in "Paria" on which we should concentrate are the ironic use of antithesis and what we might loosely term "word-play."

Tristan's constant confirmation of his status as outcast and failure is curiously reflected by a pattern of undercutting soon apparent to the careful reader. In the first stanza, he deflates the so-called freedom of the new Republican government:

> Qu'ils se payent des républiques,
> Hommes libres!—carcan au cou—
> Qu'ils peuplent leurs nids domestiques! . . .
> —Moi je suis le maigre coucou.

> From the Republic let them have the best,
> These free men—their necks in chains—
> Let them people their domestic nests! . .
> Me, I'm the skinny cuckoo they all disdain.

Here, the word-play, or rather "bird play," consists of the juxtaposition of the figurative "nids domestiques"—the hearth which shelters the bourgeois propagative fires—and the bird with which

Corbière identifies himself, the cuckoo, which has no home but, a vagrant like Tristan, lays its eggs in the nests of other ("domestic") species. Tristan is, further, a "thin" cuckoo, apparently eggless.

In regard to the pattern of irony mentioned above, this stanza is exceptional in the context of the poem because the verses in which the antithesis is stated—in this case, the bourgeois illusion of freedom is undermined ("Qu'ils se payent des républiques,/Hommes libres!—carcan au cou—")—open the quatrain (the poem, in fact). Thereafter, by contrast, it is the final two verses of nearly every stanza which constitute an antithetical undercutting. Corbière makes this formal contrast, we must suppose, in order to differentiate the Republican "nonfreedom" (stanza 1) from his own. Tristan is thus a true pariah, since he experiences even this negative trait differently than do others.

The antitheses by which Corbière undermines his own potential happiness or stability are expressed in the form of paradox or tautology. In the second stanza, the illusory freedom of the bourgeois household, contrasted with his solitary liberty, is at least a collective one, not coveted by Tristan, but shared nonetheless:

> —Moi,—cœur, eunuque, dératé
> De ce qui mouille et ce qui vibre . . .
> Que me chante leur Liberté,
> A moi? toujours seul. Toujours libre.

> —Me, —eunuch heart, spleened
> Of what moistens and what trembles for me . . .
> Their Freedom? What does it mean
> To me? Always alone. Always free.

Tristan seems to be hovering between individualistic bravado and plaintive estrangement; one thing is sure, however—the tone is typically ironic, not morose. In the following stanza, the failure to emote is replaced by the absence of a home, recalling the cuckoo passage of the opening stanza, as well as, perhaps, Camus's "patrie perdue" of which, owing to the intrinsic nature of his isolation, Corbière was never deprived:

> —Ma Patrie . . . elle est par le monde;
> Et, puisque la planète est ronde,
> Je ne crains pas d'en voir le bout . . .

Ma patrie est où je la plante:
Terre ou mer, elle est sous la plante
De mes pieds—quand je suis debout.

—My Homeland . . . it's where the world is found;
And, since the planet is round,
I have no fear of seeing its tip . . .
My country is where I stake my pole:
Land or sea, it's under the sole
Of my feet—when I'm standing up.

Related to this stanza, a deeper paradox, which transcends the poem itself, is that "Paria" is the final text of *Raccrocs ("Flukes")*, itself the last of those sections in *Les Amours jaunes* which represent the truly ironic, self-abasing Corbière *(Ça, Les Amours jaunes, Sérénade des Sérénades, Raccrocs)*. *Raccrocs* is followed by precisely the two sections *(Armor, Gens de mer)* which present us with Corbière's only feelings of a homeland and "roots" (his native Brittany, a motif to be discussed in chapter 5). The antithesis represented by the final two verses is not between opposite entities (cf. freedom/solitude), but between the reader's expectation (the movable *terra firma* homeland of a happy-go-lucky vagabond) and what is actually stated (the tautology, "elle est sous la plante/De mes pieds—quand je suis debout," which renders inane any potential statement of "sincerity").

But Corbière is not quite finished with his verbal games: the apparent tautology of stanza 3 is now qualified:

Quand je suis couché: ma patrie
C'est la couche seule et meurtrie
Où je vais forcer dans mes bras
Ma moitié, comme moi sans âme;
Et ma moitié: c'est une femme . . .
Une femme que je n'ai pas.

—My country, when I'm prone
Is my bed, battered and alone
Where I'll take to my breast
My other half, like a soulless me;
And this half: it's a girl, you see . . .
A girl who doesn't exist.

If, standing up, Corbière's home is everywhere, that is to say nowhere (since, by definition, a homeland is localized and exists only in contrast to lands which are "foreign"), his prone plight is no better. Affirming his self-portrait as a "cœur eunuque" in stanza 2, Corbière has no partner in bed—neither true "patrie" nor "nid domestique" is possible—and lacks even the powers of propagation possessed by the most normal of bourgeois men. But it is the paradoxical final verses which complete this portion of Corbière's ironic self-portrait (and the stanza): Tristan first posits the possibility of sexual fulfillment (Woman is the "body" part of the soul/body dialectic: "moi sans âme"), which, even though it contradicts the earlier verse ("la couche seule et meurtrie"), is nevertheless presently retracted a second time in the stanza's final verse, "Une femme que je n'ai pas" (again, the "eunuch" motif, as Corbière is left only "half a man"). The construction of the final two verses of the next stanza is parallel to these: "Et le mal du pays me ronge . . . /Du pays que je n'ai pas vu" ("And homesickness torments me . . . / A home I haven't seen"). If the "half" of Corbière represented by the woman disappears in the preceding stanza, the home missed by Corbière does likewise. What occurs here is a double-entendre which may have gone unnoticed at first reading: "mal du pays" may mean "homesickness" or, by ellipsis, the expression "mal du" may refer to the "pain at *not* having a home," as is apparent in the subsequent verse.

In stanza 8, even Tristan's poetry is emptiness:

> Ma pensée est un souffle aride:
> C'est l'air. L'air est à moi partout.
> Et ma parole est l'écho vide
> Qui ne dit rien—et c'est tout.

> My thought is an arid breath:
> It's air. Air is in my very call.
> And my oice is the echo of death
> Which says nothing—and that's all.

The expression "et c'est tout" normally means "and that's all I have to say." But a second meaning of this expression reinforces the paradoxical facet of Tristan's person with which we are now so well acquainted: saying nothing, as a poet, is *all* he is capable of doing. Of course, we know better, since, as was the case in "Ça?" and

"Épitaphe" in particular, Tristan, despite disavowing any poetic talent whatsoever, is nevertheless expressing this idea within the confines of a poem—and a clever poem at that. The permanency of the paradox is further demonstrated in the alternating thematic pattern of the entire stanza: beginning on a note of plenitude ("pensée"), there follows a continual flow between nothingness and infinity ("aride–partout–echo vide," "rien-tout"). Again, these seemingly distraught and nonchalant statements are both true and false simultaneously: the reader should never lose sight of the paradoxical nature of Corbière's verse—its humor and pathos, its poetry and nonpoetry.

The following stanza, which deals with the poet's temporal disorientation, contains the most extensive use of paradox in the entire poem:

> Mon passé: c'est ce que j'oublie.
> La seule chose qui me lie
> C'est ma main dans mon autre main.
> Mon souvenir—Rien—C'est ma trace.
> Mon présent, c'est tout ce qui se passe
> Mon avenir—Demain . . . demain

> What I forget: that's my past.
> The only thing that holds me fast
> Is my hand which the other has borrowed.
> My memory—Nothing—That's my trace.
> My present, it's all that takes place
> My future—Tomorrow . . . tomorrow

In the initial verse, Corbière once again cleverly reverses the reader's expectations: the poet's past is not what he remembers (precisely the theme of so many Romantic poets: cf. Lamartine's "Le Lac," Musset's "Souvenir," and Hugo's "Tristesse d'Olympio," perhaps the most celebrated among many, many others), but what he *forgets*. In vv. 2–3, the only link with the world accessible to Corbière is not a spiritual one (suggested by the verb *lier*), but, ironically, a physical one—with himself, no less, and not someone else. Past, present, and future are then perfunctorily dismissed in order, with the typical Corbiérian flippancy. Echoing the "rien/tout" paradox, the fourth verse offers the "Nothing" which the poet's memory represents as his "trace," what people will remember (i.e., forget! ) him for. Finally, two tautological statements complete the stanza. If the past is simply a void for Tristan, neither present nor future holds anything special for him as well, but are simply *defined* as what they are. What is to be inferred is that his present is so meaningless as to hold no future, and his future cannot be characterized in terms of substantive dreams (cf. the "songe/ Creux," the "empty dream," of the fifth stanza) or aspirations, but, tautologically, as simply the day after the present.

Besides this series of antitheses which provides the reader with the poem's ironic base, there are various uses of word-play which Corbière, as always, is careful to cultivate while berating himself on the "superficial" thematic level. In addition to the "bird-play" (stanza 1) and double-entendre ("mal du pays," stanza 5; "tout," stanza 8) already discussed, Corbière is elsewhere—at least in these stanzas chosen for examination—preoccupied with the effects of his poetic language.

The embellishment of the onomatopoetic effects of word combinations, and especially the ascribing of a mimetic relationship between sound patterns and actual phenomena (e.g., "hissing" *s*'s, limpid *l*'s), is truly one of the most scandalous abuses of textual criticism. What occurs with the word combinations of the first two stanzas of "Paria" is something quite different—it is not onomatopoeia at all, but what we might call "cacophonic isolation." Within vv. 2–5, there is a particularly cacophonic combination of [k] sounds (eight in all) and vowel sounds which may be represented phonetically in the following way: k-k-ku/k/ku-ku/koe-ə-y-kə. Rather than ascribe a particular phenomenological value to these letters, we *can* say, to begin with, that it is certainly not by chance that these sounds are placed where they are in the text. On closer examination, we notice that between the "coucou" of v. 4 and the "eunuque" of v. 5 (significantly, the two words succinctly describe Corbière's isolated status as [non-] human being), in the space of seven syllables, there is an extraordinary concentration of cacophony, except for one word isolated amidst all the commotion: "Moi." A "real" poet might have made the attempt to avoid the enunciation of the pronoun, leaving only its metaphorical representations ("coucou," "cœur eunuque") on the page. But for Corbière, there often seems to be a certain exhibitionism, a pointing toward himself as the topic of conversation (so different from the trend of

"universalizing" in much nineteenth-century verse which preceded). The "Moi," moreover, is isolated not only by its contrasting
sound, but also (and it would be difficult to find many examples of
this phenomenon elsewhere) by *four* punctuation marks: a period
and dash before, a comma and dash after. So it is not only by overt
means (the denotative sense of the words themselves), but also
implicitly by the use of sound patterns and contrastive punctuation,
that Corbière's self-portrait as pariah is effected.

Aside from the typical playful tendency of word couplings (e.g.,
"plante–plante/De mes pieds," "couché-couche"), we see word-play
of another kind, in v. 5: "—Moi,—cœur eunuque, dératé." The
aberrancy from normal usage resides, first, in the spiritual/physical
alliance of the substantive "cœur" and the adjective "eunuque,"
implying a kind of sentimental emasculation. This combination is all
the more noticeable because we might have expected to see the
substantive followed by another adjective, "unique" (in the Romantic mode), which, phonetically related to "eunuque," thus produces
a typically Corbiérian pun. Second, this alliance is followed by the
word "dératé" (as substantive or adjective), which normally means
"(de-) spleened" (spleens of horses, according to the *Robert* dictionary—dogs, according to *Littré*—were removed [it turns out to be
an old wives' tale] to make them run faster) or, by extension, "alert"
or "precocious." It is indeed strange that Corbière should use this
word here, since he neither ran fast (indeed, any running would
have been difficult because of his physical condition) nor was he considered talented, much less precocious. On one level, the word
functions in another figurative sense, to be translated as something
like "deprived," since, again contrary to normal usage, it is followed
by the clause "De ce qui mouille et ce qui vibre." This refers to the
antecedent, "cœur eunuque," as the absence of tears (and perhaps
of semen) and heartbeat (and the passion of love-making) would
correspond to his emasculated heart. On a second level, however,
we may well conclude that this particular word ("dératé") was carefully chosen by Tristan (and juxtaposed with "cœur") in order to
associate, through word-play, two organs of the body—the heart and
the spleen—and thus further undermine the traditional, sentimental values which are generally ascribed to the former.

"Paria" concludes with the definitive—mortal—expulsion of the
outcast:

—Où que je meure: ma patrie
S'ouvrira bien, sans qu'on l'en prie,
Assez grande pour mon linceul . . .
Un linceul encor: pour que faire? . . .
Puisque ma patrie est en terre
Mon os ira bien là tout seul . . .

—Wherever I die: my native land,
Without the hint of a request,
Will open for my final rest . . .
No need for shroud or helping hand:
Since "home" is underground, my bone
Will get there just fine all alone . . .

With the irony we have seen throughout the poem, he turns the
"open arms" of his homeland's welcome into an invitation to burial;
his shroud is useless, since there is no one to bury him; and, as he
has already described his country (in stanza 3) as "où je la plante:/
Terre ou mer, elle est sous la plante/De mes pieds," it is only one
step, so to speak, to the grave. The poem ends on the word "seul,"
so for Tristan, there is no human solution to his solitude. There is,
however, in this final stanza, the suggestion of possible solace in
death, a theme to be developed, as we shall see, in the parts of *Les
Amours jaunes* to follow, especially in the extraordinary *Rondels
pour après*.

What may be termed the texture of "Paria" is typical of so much of
Corbière's verse: what at first glance appears to be repetitive,
amorphous, or prosaic turns out to be, after closer reading, a rather
subtle exposition of the poet's inner drama by means of a striking
idiosyncratic use of the French language. What ought to surface
from our reading of "Paria" is that, although Corbière is so patheti-
cally isolated from people, feelings, home, love, dreams, even life,
still his status as pariah/poet may well have been, while he lived, his
sole source of personal satisfaction.

## IV   *The Contumacious Poet*

"Le Poète contumace," one of Corbière's finest poems, is an even
more poignant example of his conception of Self as pariah, probably
because it is one of the rare instances in his verse—other examples
are "Le bossu Bitor" and "La Rapsode foraine et le pardon de
Sainte-Anne"—in which he attempts to create a dramatic context by

maintaining a somewhat coherent and recognizable narrative thread. Atypical of Corbière's (lack of) structure, it nevertheless contains many of his inimitable stylistic traits. Again, it has escaped any previous detailed textual examination: like that of "Paria," its length (176 verses) discourages such a study here as well, but a close look at key passages should suggest the poem's nature and importance.

Like two other major poems, "Épitaphe" and "Paria," "Le Poète contumace" is the concluding piece of a section, in this case, of *Les Amours jaunes* (also the title of the volume). It may be divided into three parts: stanzas 1–12 (the description of the hermit-poet's abode, of the contumacious poet himself, of his possessions—a hammock, a Breton hurdy-gurdy, a mutt named "Fidèle," and another "faithful" companion, Boredom—and of his solitary thoughts); stanzas 13–29 (the transcript of a letter the poet composes to "Elle," the elusive Female, his potential [but imagined] companion whom he implores to join him in his solitude); and stanza 30 (conclusion).

The poem opens with a typical "stage direction," stating the geographical setting: "Sur la côte d'ARMOR.—" ("On the coast of AR-MORICA.—"). What is striking here is the physical isolation, on the written page, of this phrase: the remainder of the stanza is a long, winding sentence describing the poet's abode:

> Un ancien vieux couvent,
> Les vents se croyaient là dans un moulin-à-vent,
> Et les ânes de la contrée,
> Au lierre râpé, venaient râper leurs dents
> Contre un mur si troué que, pour entrer dedans,
> On n'aurait pu trouver l'entrée.

> An ancient convent of old,
> Which felt like a mill to the winds, it is told,
> And the asses of the country,
> On the shabby ivy, used to give their teeth a good grind
> Against a wall so breached you couldn't find,
> In order to enter . . . the entry.

The implication of this scriptural separation is that, paradoxically, even in his native Brittany, Tristan (and there is no doubt that he is, in fact, the poem's protagonist) is a pariah, regarded by the *gens du pays* as "plutôt un Anglais . . . *un Être*" ("rather a Briton . . . *a Thing,*" v. 26). What becomes immediately apparent is the recognizable Corbiérian mixture of pathos and humor. On one level, the words *tell* us of the dilapidated former convent, wind whipping through it, asses grinding their teeth against it, its walls riddled with holes. But beneath the narrative level, Tristan is again playing word-games; and what transpires in this stanza is a fine example of the way in which his poetic mind works. The initial expression, "Un ancien vieux couvent," is the source of a series of word- and sound-manipulations which will continue throughout the entire stanza. We may first ask why he chose "ancien( . . . )couvent." Ordinarily, this question of choice might not arise, since, although the poet has a number of possible descriptive expressions at his disposal, we usually trust his judgment, reasoning that *this* choice was just as viable as any other. But if we take this for granted, we may miss the ludic level of communication. The expression "couvent," for one thing, allows Tristan to insert the anteposed adjective "vieux" in between, creating a second meaning for "ancien" (it is now juxtaposed with "vieux"): it can mean both "former" and "ancient"—the edifice is, thus, *really* old. More important, the constituent sounds of "couvent"—[k], [u], and [vā]—are repeated throughout the stanza, not only for their sounds, but as a series of phonic interweavings: "contrée-contre"; "troué-trouver" ("troué" also evokes "trouée," an opening, which announced the "entrée" of v. 6); and "couvent-vents-moulin-à-vent." (In addition to these are "râpé [worm]-râper [grind]" and "entrer-entrée"). "Vent" will reappear later as "rafale" (v. 34) and "vent" (v. 53), and "trou" will become a motif (with "hibou") three stanzas later. So, what would seem to be ordinary narrative poetry is transformed into a verbal adventure, with words and sounds creating their *own* story.

This technique of word-play recurs throughout the poem, as it does in much of Corbière's verse. The fourth stanza (stanzas 2–3 continue the description of the "couvent") is no exception:

> —Aujourd'hui l'hôte était de la borgne tourelle,
> Un Poète sauvage, avec un plomb dans l'aile,
> Et tombé là parmi les antiques hiboux
> Qui l'estimaient d'en haut.—Il respectait leurs trous,—
> Lui, seul hibou payant, comme son *bail* le porte:
> *Pour vingt-cinq écus l'an, dont: remettre une porte.*—

> Today, as its host, the one-eyed turret had
> A solitary Poet, with a wing full of lead,
> Who had landed there among the ancient owls
> Who appraised him from above.—He respected their holes,—
> He, the only paying owl, as his *lease* calls for:
> *For twenty-five crowns a year, plus: replace the door.*—

On the "story-line" level, the poet is described as a pitiful being, living not with people, but with owls (a traditional Celtic symbol of foreboding, they reappear, for instance, in "Nature morte"). On the lexical level, three expressions again illustrate the conscious attempt on Corbière's part to manipulate simple denotative functions. Let us first consider "la borgne tourelle." The turret has a "fenêtre borgne" which lets light in, but blocks any view to the outside. The poet is, thus, truly exiled, without contact with life outside his domicile (already described in stanza 2 as a "dungeon"). But "borgne" also functions as personification: the turret is one-eyed, just as the solitary dungeon is "Crénelé comme la mâchoire d'une vieille" ("Crenelated like an old woman's jaw"), the village priest suspects the poet to be "un lépreux" ("a leper"), and the poet is fond of "les beaux pays malsains" ("beautiful unwholesome lands"). Thus, on closer reading, "borgne" becomes part of a network of expressions of debilitation and disease which circumscribe his existence. (This "condition" has positive value as well, to be discussed in chapter 5.) Next, the poet has "un plomb dans l'aile": this is a renovation of the cliché "avoir du plomb dans l'aile" ("to be wounded" or, figuratively, "compromised" in some way). The significance of this expression is three-fold. First, by singularizing *(un)* the partitive of the original expression *(du)*, it sets the poet further apart as an aberrant creature. Second, it playfully suggests not only the figurative sense (his being "shot down" or somehow defective), but the literal sense as well: he is more "owl" than "human." In fact, he *is* one of the owls—"Lui, seul hibou payant"—and has "fallen" ("tombé") among them, both by chance and by "descent" as a result of the imaginary hunter's gunshot. Furthermore, "plomb" echoes the "aplomb" of the second stanza (the "rare aplomb" of the dungeon), which might at first appear to the reader as a rather trite description, a cliché in its own right. Finally, the expression "en haut"—i.e., the position from which the owls ("antique," like the "ancient" convent they inhabit) "appraised" the poet ("esteemed" is a second meaning, corresponding to his "respect" for them)—is complemented in the next stanza by its antithesis, "en bas":

> Pour les gens du pays, il ne les voyait pas:
> Seulement, en passant, eux regardaient d'en bas,
> 　　　Se montrant du nez sa fenêtre;

> He never saw his neighbors: although
> Passing by, they used to look from below,
> 　　　Pointing to his window with upturned nose;

So, the poet is even further isolated—between the owls looking down and the curious "uplookers."

After further description of the poet in the next two stanzas—he is suspected of "living in sin" with his Muses—Corbière inserts an incongruous octosyllabic quatrain (almost all the other verses are alexandrines):

> Faisant, d'un à-peu-près d'artiste,
> Un philosophe d'à peu près,
> Râleur de soleil ou de frais,
> En dehors de l'humaine piste.

> Letting a sort-of-philosopher take the place
> Of an artist . . . sort of,
> Finding both sun and breeze abortive,
> Outside of the human race.

Again, the immediate meaning of the stanza is clear—a simple description of a dilettante recluse. But the use of stanzaic form, specific expressions, and elliptical phrasing illustrates the very dilettantism being described explicitly: the stanza (as well as others in the poem) not only recalls, but even *echoes* other poems written by Corbière. A very "unprofessional" phenomenon indeed, usually shunned by poets, who would not dare repeat identical material: again, Corbière separates himself from the *vulgus*. The three poems echoed are "Épitaphe" (also in octosyllables), "Une mort trop travaillée," and "Sous un portrait de Corbière." The following schema reflects this interchange cultivated by our "nonpoet"; the column on the left represents verses appearing throughout "Le Poète contumace," and the one on the right includes parallel verses found in the other three texts (abbreviated as *E*, *MTT*, and *SPC*):

| | |
|---|---|
| Faisant, d'un à-peu-près d'artiste, | 1–4 *(MTT)* |
| Un philosophe d'à peu près | 19–21 *(E)* |
| | 1–3, 21 *(SPC)* |
| Se mourant en sommeil, il se vivait en rêve | 1–2 *(E)* |
| Lui, ce viveur vécu, revenant égaré, | 17–18 *(E)* |
| —Manque de savoir-vivre extrême—il survivait— | 57–8 *(E)* |
| Et—manque de savoir-mourir—il écrivait: | |
| Dans mes dégoûts surtout, j'ai des goûts élégants; | 47 *(E)* |
| Comme mes volets en pantenne, | 6–8 *(SPC)* |
| Bat, tout affolé sous l'haleine | |
| Des plus bizarres courants d'air. | |

The first part of the poem ends with the poet sitting down to write a letter to the "Elle" mentioned above: "—Manque de savoir-vivre extrême—il survivait—/Et—manque de savoir-mourir—il écrivait:" ("—For lack of knowing how to live—he survived—/And—for lack of knowing how to die—he inscribed:").

Part II (stanzas 13–29), the letter being composed, is the most prolonged statement of Corbière's inner reflections to be found in his verse. After explaining his pitiful situation ("—La chose est sûre/C'est bien moi, je suis là—mais comme une rature," "It's sure/It is I, I'm there—but as an erasure"), the poet haltingly implores his woman ("l'Absente," "the Absent One") to come join him (stanza 17):

"Reviens m'aider: Tes yeux dans ces yeux-là! Ta lèvre
Sur cette lèvre! . . .Et là, ne sens-tu pas ma fièvre
—Ma *fièvre de Toi?* . . .—Sous l'orbe est-il passé
L'arc-en-ciel au charbon par nos nuits laissé?
Et cette étoile? . . .—Oh! va, ne cherche plus l'étoile
    Que tu voulais voir à mon front;
    Une araignée a fait sa toile,
    Au même endroit—dans le plafond."

"Come back and help me: Your eyes in these eyes! Your lips
On these! . . .And don't you see how I flip
—*For You?* . . .—Have you wondered
If it's our nights that have turned the rainbow into cinders?
And that star? . . .—Oh! come on, let your search for that star ebb,
    The star you would see on my brow;
    A spider has made its web,
    In the same place—on the ceiling: look now!"

This impassioned ambivalence (cf. the next stanza: "Je suis un ét-ranger.—Cela vaut mieux peut-être . . ./—Eh bien! non, viens encor un peu me reconnaître," "I'm a stranger.—That's better per-chance . . ./But no, come back and give it a chance") is accom-panied by the familiar word-play which consists of connotations or sounds evoking subsequent expressions. There is a thread of motifs and repeated sonority which goes from "yeux" (the imagined "look of love") to "front" and "orbe" ("orbit," which recalls "orbite," "orbit," as well; or "eye socket") to "arc-en-ciel" to "étoile" to "toile." Instead of the "starry eyes," "l'Absente" will find only a spider web on the poet's "ceiling." We may recall a similar image in the third stanza of Baudelaire's "Spleen *(Quand le ciel bas et lourd . . .)*"; but whereas Baudelaire's image ("un peuple muet d'infâmes araignées/Vient tendre ses filets au fond de nos cerveaux," "a silent horde of vile spiders/Comes to spin its webs in the depths of our brains") is somber and dramatic—coming at the climax of a sinuous, suspenseful sentence and just before the sounding of the funeral bells—Corbière's serves to undercut a potentially dramatic confrontation and, like the word-game in which it takes part, again reflects a ludic rather than a lyric motivation. In fact, it may even recall the colloquial expression, "avoir une araignée dans le plafond," "to have bats in the belfry."

Two stanzas later, the poet continues his plea; here, Corbière's device of undercutting by contradiction or antithesis (most obvious in poems like "Ça?" and "Épitaphe") is prominent:

> De ta chambre,
> Tu verras mes moissons—Nous sommes en décembre—
> Mes grands bois de sapin, les fleurs d'or des genêts,
> Mes bruyères d'Armor . . .—en tas sur les chenets.
> Viens te gorger d'air pur—Ici j'ai de la brise
> Si franche! . . .que le bout de ma toiture en frise.
> Le soleil est si doux . . .—qu'il gèle tout le temps.
> Le printemps . . .—Le printemps n'est-ce pas tes vingt ans.
> On n'attend plus que toi, vois: déjà l'hirondelle
> Se pose . . . en fer rouillé, clouée à ma tourelle.—
> Et bientôt nous pourrons cueillir le champignon . . .
> Dans mon escalier que dore . . . un lumignon.
> Dans le mur qui verdoie existe une pervenche
> Sèche.—. . . Et puis nous irons à l'eau *faire* la planche
> —Planches d'épave au sec—comme moi—sur ces plages.

La Mer roucoule sa *Berceuse pour naufrages;*
Barcarolle du soir . . . pour les canards sauvages."

                                From your room,
You'll see my harvests: golden flowers of broom,
My great fir forests—December's the month—
And my Armorican briar . . .—piled up in the hearth.
Come gorge yourself on pure air.—The breeze is so cool
That even the edge of my roof becomes curled.
The sun is so nice . . .—that it's freezing forever.
The spring . . .—aren't your twenty years spring fever?
All I need is you, see: the swallow already
Is perching . . . in rusty old iron, to my turret nailed steady.—
And soon to mushroom-hunting ourselves we'll abandon . . .
On my staircase illuminated . . . by a candle-end.
A periwinkle exists on the wall so dank
Dry.—. . . . And then we'll go *float* like planks
—Shipwreck planks—like me—on these banks.
The Sea coos its *Shipwreck Lullaby;*
Evening barcarolle . . . for wild ducks that fly by."

December harvests, freezing sun, rusty swallow, rancid mushrooms, desiccated periwinkle, floating-wreck: the promise of Nature, beauty, and fun is consistently perverted by expressions of fatality or decadence. Even spring is emptied of its promise, not by contradiction, but by a rhetorical question only included in the verse for its flippant assonance, somewhat reminiscent of Guillaume Apollinaire: "Le printemps . . .—Le printemps n'est-ce pas tes vingt ans."

Stanzas 21–27, the frenzied amorous fantasies and disillusionments of the solitary poet, may well be the most strikingly dramatic and pathetic ones Corbière ever wrote. After fantasizing about what the nights of love would be like, the poet hears a knocking at the door—alas! only a rat. (Aside from the obvious dramatic disappointment, we must suppose that the owls must be nourished somehow. . . .) "Elle" (now "Toi") appears everywhere: in his solitude, his owls, his weathervane, the wind. The passage ends with the poet's hope of seeing his lady dashed by the inexorable reality of his solitude and by the only being who will ever share his bed with him, his mutt, "Faithful":

"Tiens . . . une ombre portée, un instant, est venue
Dessiner ton profil sur la muraille nue,
Et j'ai tourné la tête . . .—Espoir ou souvenir—
*Ma sœur Anne, à la tour, voyez-vous pas venir?* . . .

—Rien!—je vois . . . je vois, dans ma froide chambrette,
Mon lit capitonné de *satin de brouette;*
Et mon chien qui dort dessus—Pauvre animal—
. . . Et je ris . . . parce que ça me fait un peu mal."

"Look . . . a shadow for an instant comes to call
And trace your profile on the naked wall,
And I turned my head . . .—Hope or a mere
Memory—*Ma Sœur Anne, à la tour, voyez-vous pas venir?* . . .

—Not a thing!—I see . . . I see in my cold little room,
My bed padded with *satin of gloom;*
And my dog—Poor beast—who's asleep on it
. . . And I laugh . . . because that hurts me a bit."

If the entire passage is, as we have noted above, somewhat pathetic, it is rescued from bathos or insipidity by the poignancy of Corbière's wit, yet another illustration, by performance, of an explicit statement ("Et je ris . . .parce que ça me fait un peu mal"). The initial stanza of the passage will give us an idea of what Tristan is up to:

—"Et nos nuits! . . . *Belles nuits pour l'orgie à la tour!* . . .
Nuits à la Roméo!—Jamais il ne fait jour.—
La Nature au réveil—réveil de déchaînée—
Secouant son drap blanc . . .éteint ma cheminée.
Voici mes rossignols . . .rossignols d'ouragans—
Gais comme des poinçons—sanglots de chats-huants!
Ma girouette dérouille en haut sa tyrolienne
Et l'on entend gémir ma porte éolienne,
Comme saint Antoine en sa tentation . . .
Oh viens! joli Suppôt de la séduction!"

—"And our nights! . . . *Belles nuits pour l'orgie à la tour!* . . .
Nights like Romeo's!—Daybreak nevermore.—
Nature awakening—awakening unleashed—
Puts out the fire . . .throwing off its white sheets.
Here are my nightingales . . .hurricane nightingales—
Gay as awls—sobs of screech owls!

My weathervane shakes the rust off its yodeling song
And my Aeolian door groans the whole night long,
Like Saint Anthony in his temptation . . .
Oh come! lovely Agent of seduction!"

We notice several familiar techniques, used here by Tristan to undermine any serious notion of romanticism or sexual fulfillment: melodramatic punctuation, undercutting (in vv. 4–6 of the stanza), renovation of cliché ("Ma girouette dérouille" rewords the French aphorism "L'homme est comme une girouette; il ne se fixe que rouillé": "Man is like a weathervane; he only stops when rusty"; and "porte éolienne," "wind-door"—we recall that the poet had to replace the missing door, according to his lease—is inserted in place of the expected "harpe éolienne," the harmonious "wind-harp"), and "refined" literary allusions (*"Belles nuits pour l'orgie à la tour,"* from Dumas *père's La Tour de Nesle;* Shakespeare's Romeo; Saint Anthony). The latter is, in fact, a leitmotif, reappearing in stanzas 13 ("Je rime, donc je vis," a perversion of Descartes), 19 (Bernardin de Saint-Pierre's *Paul et Virginie,* Defoe's *Robinson Crusoe*), 23 (Nodier's *Inès de las Sierras*), and 26 (Perrault's *Barbe-Bleue*).

The letter comes to a desperate conclusion, punctuated by the familiar word-play (antithesis, pun):

"J'ai pris, pour t'appeler, ma vielle et ma lyre,
Mon cœur fait de l'esprit—le sot—pour se leurrer . . .
Viens pleurer, si mes vers ont pu te faire rire;
    Viens rire, s'ils t'ont fait pleurer . . ."

"Ce sera drôle . . .Viens jouer à la misère,
D'après nature:—*Un cœur avec une chaumière.*—
. . .Il pleut dans mon foyer, il pleut dans mon cœur feu.
Viens! Ma chandelle est morte et je n'ai plus de feu . . ."

"I have taken, to call you, hurdy-gurdy and lyre.
For deception—the dunce—my heart is a wit . . .
Come cry, if your laughs my verse can inspire;
    Come laugh, if it makes you cry over it . . ."

"It'd be funny if we played 'Misery' there.
From nature:—*Un cœur avec une chaumière.*—
There's rain on my hearth and my heart, where it's night.
Come! My candle's burned out and I haven't a light."

The final two verses are worth noting. The rain in the poet's deceased heart, a poignantly ingenious variation of the Romantic "pathetic fallacy," has been compared to Verlaine's famous *Ariette III* (from *Romances sans paroles*): "Il pleure dans mon cœur/Comme il pleut sur la ville" ("It cries in my heart/As it rains on the town"). This is just another in a series of attempts to pass off the relatively unknown Corbière's verse as a borrowing from a celebrated contemporary: as is often the case, "influence" is impossible, since Verlaine's poem (1874) appeared after Corbière's. The subsequent verse, an allusion to the popular "Pierrot" song, "Au clair de la lune," echoes two prior verses (stanza 20)—"J'ai le clair de la lune,/Et des amis pierrots amoureux sans fortune"— and establishes a precedent of "stealing" from popular tunes later practiced by two poets influenced by Corbière, Jules Laforgue and T. S. Eliot.

The final stanza of "Le Poète contumace" represents Part III, the conclusion:

> Sa lampe se mourait. Il ouvrit la fenêtre.
> Le soleil se levait. Il regarda sa lettre,
> Rit et la déchira . . . Les petits morceaux blancs,
> Dans la brume, semblaient un vol de goëlands.
>
> His light was fading. He opened the window wide.
> The sun was rising. His letter he spied,
> Laughed and tore it up . . .The little white
> Pieces, in the mist, seemed like seagulls in flight.

Having completed the long letter at dawn, the poet laughs, rips it up, and tosses it into the Breton mist. The conclusion is ironic: the letter, destroyed, is given life (it soars like so many seagulls), whereas Tristan, like Baudelaire's albatross, is a wounded bird, the owl with "lead in his wing." One critic interprets the destruction of the letter as the destruction of the poet's Self:

At the end, when the poet tears up his letter, that is, the poem which we have just read, he tears himself up, since it represents his last hope of living and of knowing himself; with it the last tie which might bind him to others is cut. At the end of solitude there is death, and Corbière knows that he can only die alone.[3]

Yes, the poet *will* die alone, but what should not be forgotten is that the letter is, in fact, *not* destroyed, but rather included in the poem which we have just read and examined. In other words, the poet *as lover* is dead, but *as poet*, he is still kicking.

The final touch is the poem's subscription: "Penmarc'h—jour de Noël" ("Penmarc'h—Christmas day"), recalling the Tristan of legend. Again, the motif of death is evoked, but what is essential is that the name *Tristan*, the "real" poet's pseudonym, remains as the final reminder of the poet's exile from literary tradition,[4] of his isolation from any community of poets, which, of course, has just been so ably illustrated by the writing of this remarkable poem.

## V  *Deaf-man's Rhapsody*

If "Le Poète contumace" is Corbière's most poignant expression of a spiritual and emotional isolation from his milieu, "Rapsodie du sourd" is the most profound metaphorical statement of a physical disability which is the source of the same "separation syndrome." Metaphorical, because what is in question is not Tristan's deafness as biographical fact (like everything else, impossible to prove, despite the hypothesis of Henri Thomas),[5] but his isolation from human intercourse stemming from a figurative "amputation" of his hearing. The "operation to remove his hearing" in "Rapsodie du sourd" is all the more poignant, since Tristan did indeed consider his physical impairments as the source of much of his unhappiness, and because the malefactor, in this instance, is a doctor, a "man of art" (and we know what Tristan thinks of "art") who represents a person of "correct" social stature:

> L'homme de l'art lui dit:—Fort bien, restons-en là.
> Le traitement est fait: vous êtes sourd. Voilà
> Comme quoi vous avez l'organe bien perdu.—
> Et lui comprit trop bien, n'ayant pas entendu.

> The man of art said to him:—Very well, let's leave it at that.
> The treatment is over: you're deaf. That's what
> Makes your organ nonfunctioning.—
> And he understood too well, having heard not a thing.

The remainder of the poem is basically a series of "ravings" by the poet, cut off from others by his inability to hear, doubting his own humanity and his powers of communication by means of ordinary language. At the conclusion, the poet asks his female companion (his "contemplative Idol") to join him in silence, the only alternative left and, paradoxically, the only possible method of communication.

On the surface, the poem's substance is rather pitiful. The "sourd" alternately tags himself as "mannequin muet" ("mute dummy"), "vierge" and "lépreux" ("virgin" and "leper," which we recall from "Le Poète contumace"), "Poète muselé" ("muzzled poet"), "hérisson à rebours" ("backward hedgehog"), "Tantale acoustique" ("acoustical Tantalus"), "Gobe-mouche impuissant," "Tête-de-turc-gratis" ("helpless sucker," "free scapegoat"). The fundamental statement of the poet's isolation on the human (communicative) level is clear; the ear operation would seem to be just another variation of this theme seen so often elsewhere in the volume (and just commented upon vis-à-vis "Paria" and "Le Poète contumace"). The most thorough examination of the psychological ramifications of the poet's deafness and road to mutism has been done by Keith Macfarlane; it should be consulted.[6] From this (thematic) viewpoint, little can be added, but even in this fine exegesis, the apparently "sudden" insufficiency of normal discourse seems to be concomitant with the "newly found" speech resulting from recent deafness:

the old intellectual and artistic forms—elegance, finesse, nuance, clarity, order—cultivated and present practically in the very structures of poetic thought, are condemned to remain in this potential state in the absence of a faithful vehicle which would bring them back to life. The phrase *"I speak beneath myself"* thus questions the pertinence of qualities which had become the recognizable trait of the poetic work: enclosed in the mind, unable to be realized, they remain for Tristan just so many vain forms.[7]

We should now be wise to Tristan's poetic posing, however—wise enough, at any rate, to sense that his verbal patterns have not changed and that the operation is simply a tongue-in-cheek ploy to divert the reader's attention away from a more subtle proposition: if the deaf-man (the poet-persona) is incoherent, "muzzled," and, eventually, mute (Tristan's "human" situation), Corbière, as always, has full control of his text (his "poetic" situation), creating his inimitable brand of antilyricism. Rather than examine this text from a purely thematic or psychological perspective, then, let us confine ourselves to a discussion of the stylistic features which nourish this basic paradox of communicative impotence and poetic potency. In both cases, Corbière is isolated from his milieu, but with the latter, a positive creation is extracted from a negative dilemma, just as Baudelaire "alchemically" forged the "or" ("gold") from the "boue" ("mud") of his gloomy poetic raw material.

Speaking of "or," Corbière uses this very syllable in one of several "acoustical" manipulations found throughout the poem: only the attentive reader will appreciate the fundamental irony of a deaf poet who has apparently lost control of the sounds he emits (and who, ultimately, vows himself to silence) controlling these sounds in the very poem which expresses this dilemma. Starting backwards at the final stanza (again, often a useful method when dealing with Tristan), we see the syllable in the poem's final verse:

> —Soyez muette pour moi, contemplative Idole,
> Tous les deux, l'un par l'autre, oubliant la parole,
> Vous ne me direz mot: je ne répondrai rien . . .
> Et rien ne pourra dédorer l'entretien.

> —Be mute for me, contemplative Idol,
> We'll both keep our voices bridled,
> You'll say nothing to me: the same I'll do . . .
> And nothing will tarnish our interview.

The sound "or" (here "d[']or," "golden") is echoed in the subscription which follows: "*Le silence est d'or* (Saint Jean Chrysostome)." The "golden silence" is not only ascribed incorrectly in this allusion (its source is Arabic, not "Saint John Golden-Mouth"), but the play on "or" establishes the *presence* of the word (or the sound) the *absence* of which has just been affirmed ("oubliant la parole"). Just as the written poem contradicts the tearing up of the letter at the conclusion of "Le Poète contumace," here the vow of silence is in conflict with the concluding sounds. Furthermore, if we trace the sound "or" throughout the poem we see the entity of *sound* (and not its antithesis, "golden silence") confirmed: it reappears, often in words which might easily have been overlooked in favor of synonyms or else simply omitted—F*or*t (bien), *or*gane, Dés*or*mais, *or*gueil, *or*eille, c*or*ne, and (twice) c*or*.

Sound-play, particularly significant in a poem such as this one, occurs elsewhere, notably in stanzas 2–3, 10, and 14. In the first instance, two sounds—[œ :j] and [u]—are interwoven in such a way that the words in which they appear have semantic links as well:

> —Eh bien, merci Monsieur, vous qui daignez me rendre
> La tête comme un bon cercueil.
> Désormais, à crédit, je pourrai tout entendre
> Avec un légitime orgueil . . .
>
> A *l'œil*–Mais gare à l'œil jaloux, gardant la place
> De l'oreille au clou! . . .—Non—À quoi sert de braver?
> . . . Si j'ai sifflé trop haut le ridicule en face,
> En face, et bassement, il pourra me baver! . . .

> Well, Sir, thanks a bunch for making
> My head like a nice coffin inside.
> Henceforth, on credit, I'll hear everything
> With justifiable pride . . .
>
> *For the eye*—But woe to the jealous eye, taking the place
> Of the fallow ear! . . .—No—Why persevere?
> . . . If I shout too loud at the sot across from me, in my face,
> And meanly, he could curse my ear! . . .

The rhyme "cercueil-orgueil" in the second stanza leads naturally to the "œil" which begins stanza 3. (Identical in sound, the word is used as a sensorial substitute for the now-defunct ear.) "Œil" is soon repeated as assonance, with the adjective "jaloux" appended, which is then followed by still another internal rhyme, "clou" ("nail"), which refers back semantically to the "cercueil" ("coffin," which is "nailed" shut) of v. 6. In the tenth stanza, the aural disorientation is reflected *consciously* in the text by a series of interrelated cacophonies. The opening verse is even more effective than Mallarmé's celebrated "Aboli bibelot d'inanité sonore" ("Abolished bauble of sonorous inanity") from the "Sonnet en -yx" in miming the sonorous void: "—Hystérique tourment d'un Tantale acoustique!" ("—Hysterical torment of an acoustical Tantalus! "). The [ik] sound frames the verse, and, more important, the series of [t] (five times) and [u] (twice) sounds reappear, the former in the stanza's final verse (four times), the latter in v. 3 (twice, accompanied by four cacophonous *m*'s): "Gobe-mouche impuissant, mangé par un moustique,/Tête-de-turc gratis où chacun peut taper." ("Helpless sucker, eaten by a mosquito,/Free scapegoat everyone can scorn").

In stanza 14, the [u] sound—which began in the title and first
stanza in the key word, "sourd"; continued in stanzas 2–3 (*vous-
pou*rrai- *ja*l*ou*x- cl*ou*); and reappeared throughout the entire text
(rad*ou*ci, t*ou*j*ou*rs, *ou*blié, *Ou*, m*ou*vement, s*ou*rire, c*ou*p, reb*ou*rs,
s*ou*rd, t*ou*rment, ac*ou*stique, m*ou*che, m*ou*stique, *où*, c*ou*teau,
b*ou*chon, c*ou*plet [these last three are part of the "sourd's" "celestial
music"], s*ou*s, in*dou*, b*ou*ché, tr*ou*, s*oû*l, c*ou*c*ou*, m*ou*cheron, t*ou*s,
*ou*bliant, p*ou*rra)—occurs eight times in all its cacophonous splen-
dor:

> —Va te coucher, mon cœur! et ne bats plus de l'aile.
> Dans la lanterne sourde étouffons la chandelle,
> Et tout ce qui vibrait là—je ne sais plus où—
> Oubliette où l'on vient de tirer le verrou.
>
> —Go lie down, my heart! and no more take flight.
> In the deaf lantern let's put out the light,
> And all that was moving—I don't recall where—
> Prison, and they've just bolted me there.

If there is conscious sound-play, there is also controlled word-
play. First, as so often happens, particularly in Corbière's lengthier
texts, a network of expressions is established, seemingly spontaneous associations which in fact unify the text and give it a certain
coherence. In "Rapsodie du sourd," the two associations of words
are those of *musical instruments* and *animals:* the choices are
significant, corresponding to the sound the poet has lost, and to his
dehumanization.

The instruments begin in stanza 5, with the verb *corner* (the
literal meaning is "shout," but, by connotation—it means "shout" by
extension—it suggests a "corne," or "horn"). Then come "guitare"
(in apposition to "officieux être," another "instrument" [person] unheard by the "sourd"), "trompe d'Eustache" (Eustachian tube, but
"trompe" also means "horn"), "cor" (juxtaposed with "trompe
d'Eustache," it confirms this word-play), "clarinette" (the "sourd"
doesn't know whether he's speaking "Hindi" or "duck," like the
clarinette of a stupid blind man who covers the wrong hole), "tam-
tam" (he asks the haywire balance-wheel in his head to "beat the
drum"), and the "sonnette" (his head is a "cracked cauldron" which
cannot differentiate between a woman's voice and a bell). Elsewhere
characterized as an assortment of animals (toad, dog, owl, etc.), the

poet's soul is here an ass wearing a gray bonnet; he is then a "hérisson à rebours" (an inverted hedgehog, bristles inside); he speaks "duck-talk"; and his heart, like the owl and cuckoo in other poems, is a flying creature whose wings he entreats to cease beating and to capitulate ("—Va te coucher, mon cœur! et ne bats plus de l'aile").

In addition to these word groups, plays on words appear, typically, as further evidence of the poet's consciousness of his own language (contrary to the explicit statements of the text). Aside from the plays on "trompe d'Eustache" and *corner* mentioned above, the poem's title and second verse ("Le traitement est fait: vous êtes sourd"), expressing the basic paradox of the deaf-man's situation, are followed by another paradoxical assertion which defines the patient's apparently lucid postoperative state: "Et lui comprit trop bien, n'ayant pas entendu." But the real irony resides in the pun on the verb *entendre*, which can mean either "to hear" or "to understand": thus, the patient not only understands the results of the botching (not hearing the results *is* the results), but he understands by not understanding. He is thus isolated from humanity not only in an auditory sense, but in an intellectual one as well. Another polyvalent expression is "l'oreille au clou," figuratively connoting an ear in disuse ("nailed down"), but literally echoing the "cercueil" ("coffin") to which his head is likened. This figurative death is, again, canceled by the playfulness of the poet's expression. Finally, vv. 11–12 present the reader with two more puns: " . . . Si j'ai sifflé trop haut le ridicule en face,/En face, et bassement, il pourra me baver!" "Bassement," "in a vile manner," is also played against its opposite, "haut," of the preceding verse. "Baver," figuratively "to ridicule," also means, literally, "to drivel," which both adds an additional meaning to "en face" ("opposite," but now "in the face") and announces the old woman who, in stanza 7, comes to "saliver sa sainte compassion/Dans ma *trompe d'Eustache*" ("dribble her blessed compassion/In my *Eustachian tube*").

In an article written for the journal *Europe*, Tristan (!) Tzara, founder of the "Dada" movement, called Corbière an "exile among exiles." What the study of the poems in this chapter has thus far attempted to demonstrate is that, even beyond Tristan's physical, moral, psychological, or emotional isolation from humanity (all "negative"), what separated him from the rest—the only positive element in his pitiful existence—was his unique manner of self-expression, a style which, even while exposing this most pathetic aspect of exile and isolation, asserted itself in its typically aggressive and playful manner.

## VI  *No Iseut*

It was as if all the flowers with which Tristan had ever played that "She loves me/She loves me not" game had even-numbered petals! His failure to develop a heterosexual relationship was probably the most painful aspect of Tristan's exile from humanity and one which surely deserves further commentary.[8] The numerous poems about love and the very title of his collection (*Les Amours jaunes*, "Jaundiced Loves")[9] indeed suggest that this was one of the most important preoccupations in Corbière's verse.

Even the most isolated of Romantic heroes had at least one physical or spiritual relationship with a woman; in Tristan's case, even this most fundamental and accessible pleasure was denied him. We know that this situation was particularly painful from 1871 on, during the unrequited relationship with "Marcelle"; but we also have evidence (if we can trust the dating) that as early as 1868, Corbière had developed an ironic conception of love in which hope naturally became despair (the excerpts which follow are vv. 5–20 and 32–33 of "Sous un portrait de Corbière en couleurs fait par lui et daté de 1868"):

L'amour! . . . je l'ai rêvé, mom cœur au grand ouvert
Bat comme un volet en pantenne
Habité par la froide haleine
Des plus bizarres courants d'air;
Qui voudrait s'y jeter? . . .pas moi si j'étais ELLE! . . .
Va te coucher, mon cœur, et ne bats plus de l'aile.

J'aurais voulu souffrir et mourir d'une femme,
M'ouvrir du haut en bas et lui donner en flamme,
Comme un punch, ce cœur-là, chaud sous le chaud soleil . . .

Alors je chanterais (faux, comme de coutume)
Et j'irais me coucher seul dans la trouble brume
Éternité, néant, mort, sommeil, ou réveil.

Ah si j'étais un peu compris! Si par pitié
Une femme pouvait me sourire à moitié,
Je lui dirais: oh viens, ange qui me consoles! . . .

. . . . . . . . . . . . . . . . . . . . . . . . . . . . . . . . . . . . . . . . . . . . . . . . . . . . . .

. . .Et je la conduirais à l'hospice des folles.
[ . . . ]
Je voudrais être alors chien de fille publique,
Lécher un peu d'amour qui ne soit pas payé;

Love! . . .I have dreamed it, my heart stripped bare
Beats like a shutter not held fast
Inhabited by the cold blast
Of the most bizarre currents of air;
Who would want to throw himself into it? . . .not I if I were SHE! . . .
Go to sleep, my heart, and put your wing away for eternity.

I would have liked to suffer and die from a dame,
To have exposed myself from top to bottom and have
    given her in flames,
Like punch, this heart, hot under the sun's heat . . .

Then I would sing (off-key, as I am prone)
And go off to sleep in the troubled mist all alone
Eternity, void, death, awakening, sleep.

Ah if I were a little understood! If by pity
A woman could half-smile at me,
I would say to her: oh come, angel who consoles! . . .
. . . . . . . . . . . . . . . . . . . . . . . . . . . . . . . . . . . . . . . . . . . . . . . . . . . . . . . . . . . . . . .
. . .And to the looney bin with her I'd stroll.
[ . . . ]
So I'd like to be a wench's dog,
To lick a bit of love without a price-tag;

In terms of his personal, biographical situation, Corbière was
constantly aware that his amorous aspirations were doomed from the
start; that he would always be subjected to the vilest experiences of
humiliation and failure; that he, as Tristan, would never get his
Iseut. (The irony of his pseudonym is further apparent in his dubbing of Rodolphe de Battine as "Ménélas":[10] he was indeed incapa-
ble of separating Rodolphe from Marcelle, unlike the heroic Paris,
who abducted Menelaus's wife, Helen.) The fundamental reason for
this chronic failure was Tristan's physical appearance. Actually, if we
compare the caricatures drawn by Tristan (one may be found at the
beginning of this book) with the few photographs of the poet, we can
see to what extent Corbière exaggerated his self-perceived ugliness.
In any case, his conception of himself as a repulsive beast never
wavered, as his frequent author's signature—"une gueule," "a

mug,"—under his drawings and caricatures attests. Evidence of this aspect of his self-conception can be found throughout his verse as well. In "Guitare," he blurts out, "Je suis si laid!" The first two and last two stanzas of "Femme" express the same physical revulsion, but from the woman's standpoint:

Lui—cet être faussé, mal aimé, mal souffert,
Mal haï—mauvais livre . . .et pire: il m'intéresse.—
S'il est vide après tout . . .Oh mon dieu, je le laisse,
    Comme un roman pauvre—entr'ouvert.

Cet homme est laid . . .—Et moi, ne suis-je donc pas belle,
    Et belle encore pour nous deux!—
En suis-je donc enfin aux rêves de pucelle? . . .
    —Je suis reine: Qu'il soit lépreux!
[ . . . ]

Oui!—Baiser de Judas—Lui cracher à la bouche
    Cet *amour*!—Il l'a mérité—
Lui dont la triste image est debout sur ma couche,
    Implacable de volupté.

Oh oui: coller ma langue à l'inerte sourire
    Qu'il porte là comme un faux pli!
Songe creux et malsain, repoussant . . .qui m'attire!
. . . . . . . . . . . . . . . . . . . . . . . . . . . . . . . . . . . . . . . . . . . . . . . . . . . . . . . . . . .
    —Une nuit blanche . . .un jour sali . . .

He—this warped being, badly tolerated, badly loved, nay,
Badly hated—a bad book . . .and worse: he's not bad.—
If he's empty after all . . .I'll put him down, oh my God,
    Like a poor novel—open halfway.

This guy is ugly . . .—And I, I'm lovely, it seems,
    And lovely yet for the both of us!—
Well, even lovely enough for a virgin's dreams? . . .
    —I am queen: Let him be leprous!
[ . . . ]

Yes!—Kiss of Judas—Spit in his mouth
    This *love*!—He's deserved it all right—
He whose sad image is standing on my couch,
    Implacable with delight.

Oh yes: paste my tongue on his inert smile
    Which, like a crease, he wears that way!

Empty, dirty dream, repulsive—which attracts me all the while!
. . . . . . . . . . . . . . . . . . . . . . . . . . . . . . . . . . . . . . . . . . . . . . . . . . . . . . . . . . . . .
          —A sleepless night . . .a sullied day . . .

We can see where Apollinaire might have gotten his expression
"mal aimé"; more important, both the opening and closing stanzas
reflect the typically Corbiérian technique of ironic undercutting, in
which the door of hope ("il m'intéresse," "qui m'attire") is slammed
shut by the stark reality of the poet's repulsive physical appearance.

Another, even earlier text which rather clearly states Tristan's
"affliction" (the piece was written when Tristan was sixteen or se-
venteen) is entitled "Sous une photographie de Corbière" ("Under a
Photograph of Corbière"):

> Aïe aïe aïe, aïe aïe aïe
> Aïe aïe aïe qu'il est laid!
>           V'là c'que c'est
>           C'est bien fait
> fallait pas qu'y aille (bis)
> fair'son portrait
>
> Oo oo oo, oo oo oo
> Oo oo oo is he gross!
>           I'd like to boast
>           That he's the most
> he didn't have to go (twice)
> to take his pose

The young Corbière is said to have remarked to a servant: "Oui,
petit, regarde ma tête, et quand tu vivras cent ans, tu ne verras
jamais un animal si laid" ("Yes, little one, look at my mug, and if you
live to be a hundred, you'll never see such an ugly animal"). In
Brittany, he was known as An Ankou (the appropriately hyper-
bolic Breton expression meaning "Specter of Death"). There were
surely others in the French literary tradition who could have em-
phasized their lack of attractiveness (even if this is, admittedly, an
extremely relative and problematic area), e.g., Charles Cros, Verlaine, Cendrars, Apollinaire, Supervielle. But in the latter cases,
optimism,escape, religious conversion, or similar outlets precluded
any chronic, morose preoccupation with the problem.

But from a purely personal problem (i.e., the effects of physical
impairment on the poet's psyche, the mysterious and disastrous

relationship between Tristan and Marcelle), heterosexual love becomes, in Corbière's poetry, another facet of the exile syndrome which we have been discussing in this chapter. It is not a question, with Corbière, of a metaphysical misogyny (cf. Laforgue, Schopenhauer), but rather of another literary pose: the frustration and failure of his amorous attempts are hidden behind a mask of frivolity or irony.[11] Corbière as an entity is separated from Woman as a collective force, who is seen as an eternal adversary. In "Femme" and "Pauvre garçon," she is referred to, in the epigraphs, as *"La Bête féroce," "The Ferocious Beast."* This dualism is often "duelism," that is, love is humorously portrayed as a duel between the two antagonists, Tristan and Woman, as in "Fleur d'art," "À la douce amie," and "Féminin singulier." Although some critics insist on seeing Marcelle herself in many of these "misogynous" poems, Woman is clearly an anonymous and collective force rather than a simple biographical allusion. She is also frequently stripped of her eroticism, as Laforgue suggested:

Sensual—he never shows the flesh—miracle there is not one breast, not one boob( . . .)in his poetry.—Still fewer bellies and thighs—He only shows the sway of the hip, the hand motion, the look of the head—parasol, fan—a vague erection as barrier.[12]

Laforgue was incorrect in his boob-counting, but the breast that does appear in one of Corbière's poems is hardly erotic; rather, it appears in an ironic comparison between Mount Etna and a woman (in "À l'Etna"):

—Toi que l'on compare à la femme . . .
—Pourquoi?—Pour ton âge? ou ton âme
De caillou cuit? . . .—Ça fait rêver . . .
—Et tu t'en fais rire à crever!—

—Tu ris jaune et tousses: sans doute,
Crachant un vieil amour malsain;
La lave coule sous la croûte
De ton vieux cancer au sein.

You whom they cast in a woman's role . . .
Why?—For your age? or your soul
Of baked flint? . . .—That makes one dream . . .
—And you laugh enough to bust a seam!—

> —You laugh yellow and cough: no doubt,
> Spitting an old sick love right out;
> The lava flows beneath the crust
> Of your old cancer of the breast.

We should now take a closer look at two poems which make fun of the normal heterosexual relationship, "Sonnet à Sir Bob" and "À une camarade." In both poems, the woman is portrayed as a prostitute, which is precisely the role frequently played by Tristan's Muse. The serious intent to write poetry and the serious attempt to establish a heterosexual relationship (already seen in "Sous un portrait de Corbière," in which the woman is also described as a "fille publique" and the poet as a "chien") are both masked by this obviously abnormal or "incorrect" situation.

In "Sonnet à Sir Bob," the poet desires to change places with a mutt named "Sir Bob," so named by its mistress, a "femme légère." In a typical play on words, the poet would exchange his "sonnet" ("sonnet") for the mutt's "sonnette" ("bell," or, if there existed such a thing, the feminine form for "sonnet"). He would thus at last be the mistress's only faithful lover and would at last be able to caress a woman. If elsewhere Tristan "doggedly" attempts to dominate the woman in question, here he is content to assume the (consolation) role of servility. He has expressly chosen an animal which is passive and servile, in contrast, say, to Baudelaire's mysterious, aloof, and independent cats. In this case, the poet's irony barely hides the pitiful situation he is really experiencing. A similar domination of the poet by a prostitute has been seen in "Bonne fortune et fortune"; and, besides in "Sous un portrait," the dog-mistress relationship reappears in the final stanza of "Elizir d'amor": "Maîtresse peut me connaître,/Chien parmi les chiens perdus:" ("Mistress can know me,/Dog among lost dogs:").

"À une camarade," in which the "pal" of the title (we should notice that the poem is not dedicated to a "lover") is another "loose" woman, is perhaps the best illustration of the ironic presentation of Corbière as pitiful (non-)lover. In the first stanza, Tristan is again playing games, not only with his heart, but with his words. The pun "femme/fille" ("woman"/"girl," or "wench") and the cacophonic fourth verse attest to this:

> Que me veux-tu, femme trois fois fille? . . .
> Moi qui te croyais un si bon enfant!
> —De l'amour? . . .—Allons: cherche, apporte, pille!
> M'aimer aussi, toi! . . . moi qui t'aimais tant.

> What do you want of me, woman three times slut? . . .
> Me who believed you to be such a nice child!
> —Love? . . .—Come on, search, bring, loot!
> Love me too! . . . me whom you drove so wild.

In stanzas 2 and 4, the typical ironic undercut is employed: first, after comparing himself to a lizard (a physical parallel to dog and toad) and his "love" to a ray of light, Corbière finds Love a hindrance to his "sun-bathing" (thus, logically, his "love" is "love-less"); and next, if his love is a "rare" bauble, it nevertheless lacks the bauble's ability to be glued back together again:

> Oh! je t'aimais comme . . . un lézard qui pèle
> Aime le rayon qui cuit son sommeil . . .
> L'Amour entre nous vient battre de l'aile:
> —Eh! qu'il s'ôte de devant mon soleil!
> [ . . . ]
> —Curiosité, bibelot, bricole? . . .
> C'est possible: il est rare—et c'est son bien—
> Mais un bibelot cassé se recolle;
> Et lui, décollé, ne vaudra plus rien! . . .

> Oh! I loved you like . . . a lizard who's peeling
> Loves the ray that cooks its sleep well-done . . .
> Love comes between us beating its wing:
> —Hey! I hope he gets away from in front of my sun!
> [ . . . ]
> —Curiosity, bauble, token? . . .
> It's possible: it's rare—and that's for its own good—
> But a bauble can be glued if it's broken;
> And *it* is worthless, being unglued! . . .

An incredible innocence—another pose—marks the sixth stanza, in which the poet attempts to avoid the blame for his amorous inactivity, as if the sexual act were some kind of fight (or, as we have mentioned, a duel):

> Que nous sommes-nous donc fait l'un à l'autre? . . .
> —Rien . . .—Peut-être alors que c'est pour cela;
> —Quel a commencé?—Pas moi, bon apôtr '
> Après, quel à dira: c'est donc tour—voilà!

> What then have we done to each other? . . .
> —Nothing . . .—Well, maybe that's why we're like this;
> —Who began it?—Not me, brother!
> After, who'll say: that's all there is!

After terming his relationship, at best, "amitié calmée," "calmed friendship" (a lazy cop-out for our basking lizard), and his "friend," once again, a "mal-aimée" ("mis-loved"), Tristan ends the poem with a stanza which perverts everything. After love-making, cigarettes are typically smoked; here, where love is *not* made, a truce is the couple's only "token." If they die, it will not be from love, but from laughter. And what the poet loved about his "friend" was simply her laughter, which we can guess was sardonic (cf. "Tu ris jaune" of "À l'Etna"):

> Nous pourrons, au moins, ne pas nous maudire
> —Si ça t'est égal—le quart d'heure après.
> Si nous en mourons—ce sera de rire . . .
> Moi qui l'aimais tant ton rire si frais!
>
> The least we could do is avoid our gall
> —If that's OK with you—the quarter-hour after.
> It would be from laughter—if we die from it all . . .
> I who so loved your fresh laughter!

This ends our discussion of Corbière's estrangement from his fellow "man," particularly in the two senses of this expression, i.e., as a human being and as a being whom love normally allies with his opposite number, "woman." A passage from Keith Macfarlane's chapter on "Tristan the Lover" will serve as an excellent transition between this essential dilemma and the solutions Corbière considered, to be discussed in the chapter to follow:

Love was a human solution attempted by Tristan Corbière to resolve a difficulty foreign to recognized human norms. His experience with women helps us to appreciate the abyss which separates him morally from the rest of humanity. Condemned as he is to lead his life "outside the human path," he will have to look for his salvation in regions where few men would wish to venture. Oblivion or destruction will assuage an anguish which the purely human solution only worsened.[13]

So, if human intercourse (both social and sexual) were impossible for Corbière, perhaps solace (aside from the writing of poetry, as we have repeatedly asserted) could only come from an isolated life-situation—the quaint and mysterious qualities of his native Brittany—or else from an experience which comes after life—death itself. It is these possible sources which we shall now explore.

CHAPTER 5

# *Rule* Bretagne *and*
# *"For After . . . "*

### I Armor

A N essential aspect of Corbière's poetry which we have mentioned from the very start is its unpredictability, its surprises,
enigmas, and paradoxes. One of the more perplexing of problems
surrounding his verse concerns the final three ("Breton") sections of
*Les Amours jaunes* (the first four have been loosely termed the
"Parisian" sections)—*Armor* (Breton for "Brittany"), *Gens de mer*,
*Rondels pour après*. For one thing, the poetry itself is nearly antithetical to that contained in *Ça, Les Amours jaunes, Sérénade des
Sérénades*, and *Raccrocs;* we may at first wonder, in fact, whether
they were written by the same poet. In a word, "Tristan" disappears, the first-person perspective becoming third-person (a switch
from subjective to objective point of view); the irony is all but gone,
yielding to a tone that is rather serious, almost touching at times;
and the linguistic innovation and "trickery" are almost completely
subdued, giving way to a much tamer and more sober brand of verse
(although elements such as slang and aberrant punctuation are still
apparent). For another, the subject matter (almost too obviously)
clashes noticeably with what has preceded. It is almost as if, after
reading "Paria" (the concluding piece of *Raccrocs*), we have opened
a totally new volume of poems, left Paris (artificial) and the world of
jaundiced loves, and entered the world of Brittany (natural) and the
high seas. For the first time, Corbière's verse seems to be sincere,
optimistic, to be holding something in esteem, namely, Brittany and
its hardy inhabitants. The land and its people were both ugly and
rough-hewn, and it was these very qualities which were held in high
esteem in this region (contrary to the traditional values of beauty

127

and refinement cherished by the inhabitants of the Capital) and which doubtless struck chords of identity and compassion in Tristan.

The problem the reader faces is that, although there *seems* to be a clear "evolution" from the Paris poems to the Breton poems (i.e., from despair and self-irony to redemption and self-fulfillment), there is no way to ascertain whether Tristan intended the entire volume to be a sort of "spiritual autobiography." The "architecture" is surely less sturdy than, for instance, that of Baudelaire's *Les Fleurs du Mal,* and the "Paris" and "Breton" sections are not entirely monolithic and without examples of incongruous pieces. We should note that the Breton sections, although written *before* the others, are placed at the *end* of *Les Amours jaunes,* suggesting that Corbière may have wished to imply the importance of these texts. But the volume ends with "posthumous" poems and a desire for death (seen by some critics as a supreme liberation),[1] so we might conclude that even Brittany could not solace Corbière's aching heart and exiled status, and that the function of these poems of his homeland is not real, but ideal, not to be lived (we remember Corbière's frustrations of nonparticipation in maritime exploits), but to be pondered.

The most eloquent argument for the "bifurcation" of *Les Amours jaunes* has been presented by Albert Sonnenfeld:

In the moral structure of *Les Amours jaunes,* Paris and Brittany function above all as symbols. Paris signifies solitude and damnation; Brittany human solidarity and religious salvation.[2]

In a subsequent article which argues that for Corbière, ugliness is in reality a blessing (a "beatific malediction") and that Brittany thus represents redemption for him, Sonnenfeld continues:

In the imaginary spiritual autobiography that Corbière is writing in his *Amours jaunes,* he looks back to Brittany for spiritual redemption, for an end to his bitter loneliness. By rejoining the simple traditions of his native province, the poet can accept his ugliness (real or imagined) as a blessing, for, as Stéphane Strowski has pointed out in his sociological study, *Les Bretons,* Brittany is a land where the ugly are respected, indeed often worshiped, as holy creatures.[3]

These arguments are well taken; it would be difficult to prove, on the other hand, that Corbière had actually preconceived such a logical, demarcated, clearly defined spiritual itinerary for himself. For example, one conflicting hypothesis might be that the first four sections refer to the title of the volume and that the last three are simply a tacked-on "coda" and have little to do with the principal subject of the *recueil*, Corbière and his jaundiced loves. Furthermore, consistency, predictability, and logic were not Corbière's forte (and, in fact, were repugnant to him). At any rate, nothing will be solved here by such speculation. Let us simply examine Corbière's world of Brittany—its land and its inhabitants—to see one of the few positive, albeit idealized, values in his life. We may let our guard down for the moment, as surprise and ludicity are replaced, for the most part, by a totally different kind of poetry.

## II  Armor: *The Land*

Among the very early poems of Corbière, the pieces of *Armor* and *Gens de mer* are exceptional in their expression of a (surprisingly, if only in light of his later verse) nostalgic ideal. Although his childhood could hardly be characterized as ecstatic, Corbière was obviously attracted by the traditions, the mystery, and the "dark" aspect of his native province. This vicarious attraction—the admiration of the traditions of other times, of other people, and of a land untainted by his own personal drama—probably performed this early function of sublimation for the young Corbière. Unlike another Breton writer of the late nineteenth century, Villiers de l'Isle-Adam (who, born in Saint-Brieuc of a family of old Breton nobility, moved to Paris, frequented its literary cafés, mingled with Baudelaire, Banville, and other literati, sought fame and fortune, and generally lost his Breton identity), Tristan never lost touch with Brittany, lived there all his life, and, in fact, ordered his death-room in Morlaix to be filled with the briar which perfumed his native Armorica.

The literary influences on Corbière's Breton verse were the writings of his father, to whom he dedicated *Les Amours jaunes*, and those of his father's disciple, Gabriel de La Landelle, a poet and novelist from Morlaix, who first visited Corbière in 1862.[4] But it was the knowledge of Breton folklore, the evenings spent at Le Gad's Inn listening to yarns spun by sailors in their picturesque, argotic, maritime tongue, and his "real" existence in this region which are the fundamental sources of these poems. In them, we see a land of ancient Celtic tradition and mythology, of religious superstition and devotion, of calvaries, *cantiques*, "pardons," and crusades, standing apart with its special features of seagulls, its briar, furze, and moss, its savage heaths and rough coasts, jutting proudly into the sea like the prow of the ship "France." The topographical aspects of Tristan's Brittany, which play an important part in these final sections of *Les Amours jaunes*, are most evident in three poems, two of the land ("Paysage mauvais," "Nature morte") and one of the sea ("Au vieux Roscoff. Berceuse en Nord-ouest mineur").

What is really striking in these early poems (especially now that we have spent a good deal of time examining the innovative, ironic side of Corbière) is that they are meant to *e*voke, not to *pro*voke. The poetic language is not meant to put on an exhibition, but to be closely attuned to the subject matter it presents. Its function, in "Paysage mauvais" and "Nature morte," is to evoke the mystery, fantasy, and mythology of Brittany.

The style of "Paysage mauvais" is totally different from that of the poems in the first four sections of *Les Amours jaunes*. It is far less self-conscious, much more conservative and traditional. It is basically a kind of "tone poem" which attempts to present the mood of Brittany with its Celtic mythology, its fantasy, and its sinister qualities (hence, the unusual placement of "mauvais" after the noun in the title). Its structure is also quite different, consisting of a series of nouns (with or without verbs), one following the other, which produces the effect of cumulative description rather than the suspense, antithesis, undercutting, etc., to which we have been accustomed:

> Sables de vieux os—Le flot râle
> Des glas: crevant bruit sur bruit . . . .
> —Palud pâle, où la lune avale
> De gros vers, pour passer la nuit.
>
> —Calme de peste, où la fièvre
> Cuit . . .Le follet damné languit.
> —Herbe puante où le lièvre
> Est un sorcier poltron qui fuit . . .
>
> —La Lavandière blanche étale
> Des trépassés le linge sale,
> Au *soleil des loups* . . .—Les crapauds,
>
> Petits chantres mélancoliques,
> Empoisonnent de leurs coliques,
> Les champignons, leurs escabeaux.

> Old bony beaches—The waves cough
> Knells: bursting sound upon sound . . .
> —Pale marsh, where the moon quaffs
> Giant worms, at night, just to fool around.
>
> Calm of the plague, where
> Fever bakes . . . The cursèd sprite
> Languishes.—Stinking grass where the hare
> Is a cowardly wizard in flight . . .
>
> —The white Laundress spreads
> Out the dirty wash of the dead,
> Beneath the *wolves' sun* . . .—The toads,
>
> Little melancholic bards,
> Poison with their tubs of lard,
> The mushrooms, their stool-abodes.

This is truly the first poem we have seen so far in which the language itself does not overpower the subject matter. Here, what is engrossing is the fantastic countryside and its inhabitants: the sands, the marsh, the moon, the hare, the Laundress (in Celtic mythology, she washes the clothes of the dead), the toads (with the owl and the cuckoo, Celtic symbols of the sinister and death). The language is (for Corbière) rather traditional. We even see an example of classical inversion, in v. 10: for the rhyme "Le linge sale des trépassés" becomes "Des trépassés le linge sale." Images which evoke (rather than calling attention to themselves as linguistic entities) appear throughout: the metaphorical bone-beaches, personified waves which cough the death-knell, the moon which mysteriously swallows worms, the cooking fever, the metaphorical hare-wizard, the wolves' sun (the moon), the toad-bards, and the toad-stools (the source of this metaphor for mushrooms being etymological, taken from the Breton expression *skabellon tonsegad*). The images result, then, in the most essential expressive feature of the poem—the vibrancy, animation, and fantasy of the foreboding Breton landscape. The importance of death will become more apparent in our discussion of the *Rondels pour après,* but even in this early piece, Corbière seems to be fascinated with this aspect, the "dark" side, of his native province.

The texture of "Nature morte" is very much the same, as we witness another series of Breton symbols, perhaps less picturesque than those in "Paysage mauvais":

Des coucous l'*Angelus* funèbre
A fait sursauter, à ténèbre,
Le coucou, pendule du vieux,

Et le chat-huant, sentinelle,
Dans sa carcasse à la chandelle
Qui flamboie à travers ses yeux.

—Écoute se taire la chouette . . .
—Un cri de bois: C'est *la brouette*
*De la Mort,* le long du chemin . . .

Et, d'un vol joyeux, la corneille
Fait le tour du toit où l'on veille
Le défunt qui s'en va demain.

The cuckoos' mournful *Angelus*
Has given the cuckoo, at dusk,
To this old man's clock, quite a surprise,

And to the screech-owl, sentinel,
Candle-in-carcass, as well,
Who blazes light through his eyes.

—Hear the owl's silent hoot of sorrow . . .
—A sylvan shriek: Its *the barrow*
*Of Death,* along the way . . .

And, in joyous flight, the crow
Flies round the roof where he spies below
The dead-man who departs the next day.

The structure of "Nature morte" and the use of inversion (in the initial verse) resemble those of "Paysage mauvais." And again, picturesque imagery evoking the mood of this "still-life" (we should note the pun of the title, which may also suggest "dead nature," or the sinister aspects of Brittany) is the most prominent feature of Corbière's poetic technique. We see the cuckoo/clock announcing death; the watchful owl with fire in his eyes; the *"chouette"* (another type of owl), in a wonderful use of oxymoron (a compressed form of antithesis), hooting in silence ("Ecoute se taire"); the Death-barrow, another Breton mythological symbol; and the sinister crow spying over the dead. Because the language is more evocative than exhibitionistic, this poem is easier to "paraphrase" than any of Corbière's later pieces, but we can still enjoy the way our poet translates his fascination with Breton traditions and countryside through figurative language and realistic presentation.

Although most of the remaining poems of *Armor* portray people rather than the land itself (the "rich man," the "Rapsode foraine," the blind man, all of whom will be discussed presently), there is a poem of the sea, "Au vieux Roscoff. Berceuse en Nord-ouest mineur," which may be placed alongside "Paysage mauvais" and "Nature morte" for its evocation of the Breton countryside. Its appearance in *Gens de mer* is somewhat incongruous, since most of these poems, as the title of this section implies, are concerned with the inhabitants of Brittany, all of whom are, theoretically, "seafolk."

Stanzas 1–3, 7, and 9 illustrate how Corbière attempts to portray the ancient maritime village of Roscoff:

Trou de flibustiers, vieux nid
À corsaires!—dans la tourmente,
Dors ton bon somme de granit
Sur tes caves que le flot hante . . .

Ronfle à la mer, ronfle à la brise;
Ta corne dans la brume grise,
Ton pied marin dans les brisans . . .
—Dors: tu peux fermer ton œil borgne
Ouvert sur le large, et qui lorgne
Les Anglais, depuis trois cents ans.

Dors, vieille coque bien ancrée;
Les margats et les cormorans
Tes grands poètes d'ouragans
Viendront chanter à la marée . . .
[ . . .]

—Dors: sous les noires cheminées,
Écoute rêver tes enfants,
Mousses de quatre-vingt-dix ans,
Épaves des belles années . . .
[ . . .]

—Va: ronfle au vent, vieux ronfleur,
Tiens toujours ta gueule enragée
Braquée à l'Anglais! . . . et chargée
De maigre jonc-marin en fleur.

Pirates' den, old nest
For corsairs!—in the gale,
In your nice granite slumber, rest
On your caverns which the waves assail . . .

Snore at the sea, snore at the breeze;
Your horn in the fog as thick as peas,
Your sea-legs in the deep blue seas . . .
—Sleep; you can shut your lighthouse-eye
Opened on the deep to spy
The Limeys, for three centuries.

—Sleep, you ancient, anchored hull;
The geese and cormorants will come,
These great hurricane-poets, to strum
Their shanties to the tide when there's a lull . . .
[ . . . ]

—Sleep: under black chimneys hear
The dreams of your offspring, ahoy!
Ninety-year-old ship's-boys,
Wrecks of the good old years . . .
[ . . . ]

—Go ahead: snore at the wind, old snorer,
Always keep your angry mug held
Fixed at the Limeys! . . . and filled
With thin furze in flower.

The playful subtitle—"Berceuse en Nord-ouest mineur," "Lullaby in North-west minor"—announces the later (chronologically:
earlier, in terms of the sequence of sections in *Les Amours jaunes*),
ironic Corbière, but in a way, it is totally sincere: despite the relative harshness of the language, Corbière is singing old Roscoff to
sleep with this lovely evocation of its maritime shores. Once again,
Tristan seems to be enjoying the exercising of his poetic powers,
using a series of images to transform the town of Roscoff into a
marvelous presence. The outstanding rhetorical figure employed is
personification: Roscoff sleeps, snores, sounds its fog-horn, has
sea-legs, spies over the British with its one eye (a metaphor for its
lighthouse, but the parallel between the "deformed" Corbière and
the one-eyed Roscoff is obvious), and listens. The age and tradition
of this coastal town is evoked in the "granite slumber," the
metaphors of the "vieille coque" (Roscoff is an old ship's hull, an-

chored to the shores of France) and the "vieux ronfleur," and the "black chimneys." Adding to the local color of the scene are the "haunted caverns," the sea-birds personified into "hurricane-poets," and the metaphorical description of the old sailors as "wrecks" of days gone by. (They are thus one with their native town, which has already been likened to an old hull.)

In the light of these three early poems of the Breton countryside, we can agree with the assessment of Verlaine which appeared in the latter's *Les Poètes maudits*:

What a Breton bretoning in just the right way! Being the child of briar and great oaks and shores that he was! And how he had, this frightful false skeptic, the memory and the love of the strong superstitious beliefs of his coarse and tender coastal compatriots!

### III   Armor: *The People*

If the sinister and rugged Breton countryside and shores struck a responsive chord in Corbière he also recognized its provincial inhabitants as kindred spirits. It is just another paradox that the ugliness and crudeness which throughout his later verse was seen as the source of his suffering and isolation represent, in these early poems, qualities to be emulated and praised. But if Tristan admired these traits of his Breton compatriots so much, why did he not continue to write such verse subsequently? And why did he change his style of writing and begin to write the self-deprecating verse which represents the major portion of his poetic output? The hypothesis most readily formed is that he must have realized that while he could easily praise these qualities in his neighbors, the identification was only vicarious: for him, it could not work. For he was not one of the beggars, sailors, or blind men which he idealizes in *Armor* and *Gens de mer,* but a real person with real problems which he had to confront. Futhermore, he must have realized the transcendent importance of his poetry, its need to evolve and innovate, its function in permitting him to rise above these anonymous, idealized masses, and the nature of his ironic genius which alone could be the vehicle for the expression of his inner drama. If this kind of expression represents the "true" Corbière, we cannot, again, ignore the (perhaps sentimental) placement of these Breton poems at the end of the volume, suggesting a return to the simplicity and directness of his native background.

Unlike the sophisticated, dishonest Parisians, the Bretons were simple folk, loyal to their traditions, devout in their Celtic beliefs and religion. Above all, they were humane and compassionate. Qualities which might be scorned in the Capital—poverty, sickness, deformation, crudeness, and ugliness—were not only accepted in Brittany (as these traits were so commonplace), but revered as well, in a religious sense. As we shall see in our discussion of "La Rapsode foraine et le pardon de Sainte-Anne," even their saints shared these qualities—not afflictions—with them.

The title of one of the poems in *Armor*, "Un riche en Bretagne," typifies this attitude: the protagonist is not financially wealthy, as one might expect, but quite the opposite. He is an old beggar, a simple man who goes from door to door seeking food. He is rich, however, because he is, in his simplicity and poverty, a sort of folk-hero, revered by all: "C'est le bon riche, c'est un vieux pauvre en Bretagne, / Oui, pouilleux de pavé sans eau pure et sans ciel!" ("He's the good rich man, he's a poor old man in Brittany, / Yes, trampled from his tramping without pure water and without firmament!"). In a Eucharistic gesture, his neighbors give him the bread he desires. Above all, he does not complain about his lot, but accepts it as his natural human condition: "—Lui, n'est pas pauvre: il est Un Pauvre,—et s'en contente" ("—He's not poor: he's A Pauper,—and is content with it"). Other poems present physical deformation as heroic, or at least to be pitied. How different Tristan's attitude here is from the ironic presentation of deafness in "Rapsodie du sourd" and of ugliness in so many other poems written later! In "Cris d'aveugle," the blind man suffers and moans, but asks forgiveness and ultimately seeks redemption and solace in death:

> Pardon de prier fort
> Seigneur si c'est le sort
> Mes yeux, deux bénitiers ardents
> Le diable a mis ses doigts dedans
> Pardon de crier fort
> Seigneur contre le sort

> Forgive, if by prayers I try to sate
> Myself, Lord, if that's my fate
> My eyes, two basins blazing wide
> The devil has put his fingers inside
> Forgive me for my shouts so great
> Lord against my fate

And in "Le bossu Bitor," the deformed hunchback, a "poor little devil" who endures the most unspeakable teasing and ridicule at the hands of a group of prostitutes during a night of riotous whoring and who is driven to his death by this paroxysmal experience of humiliation and lust, is granted a final stanza of pity and the comfort of believing (even if by delusion) that he had "known love":

> Plus tard, l'eau soulevait une masse vaseuse
> Dans le dock. On trouva des plaques de vareuse . . .
> Un cadavre bossu, ballonné, démasqué
> Par les crabes. Et ça fut jeté sur le quai,
> Tout comme l'autre soir, sur une couverture.
> Restant de crabe, encore il servit de pâture
> Au rire du public; et les gamins d'enfants
> Joûant au bord de l'eau noire sous le beau temps,
> Sur sa bosse tapaient comme sur un tambour
> Crevé . . .
>               —Le pauvre corps avait connu l'amour!

> Later, the water washed up a slimy mound
> Onto the dock. Patches of jacket were found . . .
> A hunchback's body, swollen, its face gnawed away
> By the crabs. And thrown onto the quay,
> Like the other evening, on a blanket, nude.
> Abandoned by the crabs, he still served as food
> For the public's sneers; and the urchins, for a prank,
> In the nice weather, along the black water's banks,
> Beat on his hump as if it were the top of
> A broken drum . . .
>               —The wretched body had known love!

It is in "La Rapsode foraine et le pardon de Sainte-Anne," one of Corbière's finest poems, that the apotheosis of what are usually regarded as negative traits—ugliness, deformation, poverty—is most eloquently presented. The poem tells of the Breton crusaders who visit the chapel of "Sainte-Anne de-la-Palud," the patron saint of the deprived and the unfortunate. It can be divided into four parts: the introduction of the ritual of the *pardon* (stanzas 1–6), the *cantique spirituel*, or spiritual hymn sung by the people who have come for sanctification (7–29), the description of the "faithful" who have journeyed in prayer (30–49), and the characterization of the *rapsode foraine*, the "itinerant rhapsodist," a Breton character who represents salvation through her singing (50–59). Unfortunately, we do not have time to examine some of the "poetic" aspects of this long piece—its unadorned language, eloquent and reverent simplicity, and flowing rhythms—but we can take a close look at some of the qualities admiringly described by the poet. In the second part, the qualities of Sainte-Anne sung by the crusaders are quite different from those we might expect of a typical saint (purity, grace, beauty, holiness, etc.); her features are, in fact, harsh, wizened, and deformed, like those of so many of her followers:

> Mère taillée à coups de hache,
> Tout cœur de chêne dur et bon;
> Sous l'or de ta robe se cache
> L'âme en pièce d'un franc-Breton!
>
> —Vieille verte à face usée
> Comme la pierre du torrent,
> Par des larmes d'amour creusée,
> Séchée avec des pleurs de sang . . .
>
> Mother with a hatchet hewn,
> From the heart of an oak, hard and good;
> And hiding under the gold of your gown
> Is your soul, from honest Breton stock made!
>
> —Green old woman with face all worn
> Like the stone in the torrent's flood,
> By tears of love hollowed and torn,
> Wizened by tears of blood . . .

The third section offers a series of descriptions of the suffering masses, to be pitied and admired in the sense that they all reflect a certain Breton solidarity and deserve to be blessed. Not unlike their saint, they are all deformed and long-suffering; we see rachitics, epileptics, a "tronc d'homme où croît l'ulcère" ("trunk of a man where an ulcer grows"), cankerous children, lepers, cripples, and so on. But they are all faithful and, by their very humanity (the sublimated wishes of the long-suffering Tristan?), in some way divine and among the "chosen ones":

> Sont-ils pas divins sur leurs claies,
> Qu'auréole un nimbe vermeil,
> Ces propriétaires de plaies,
> Rubis vivants sous le soleil! . . .

[ . . . ]
Tas d'*ex-voto* de carne impure,
Charnier d'élus pour les cieux,
Chez le Seigneur ils sont chez eux!
—Ne sont-ils pas sa créature . . .

Aren't they divine on their trays,
All haloed in vermillion,
These proprietors of open wounds as they pray,
Living rubies under the sun! . . .
[ . . . ]
*Votive* piles of tainted meat,
Charnel-houses for heaven's elect,
At home in His house, which God will protect!
—Was their making not His own feat . . .

Finally, the *rapsode foraine* appears; her "saintly ugliness" recalls
that of Sainte-Anne:

Tu verras dans sa face creuse
Se creuser, comme dans du bois,
Un sourire; et sa main galeuse
Te faire un vrai signe de croix.

You will see in her face all hollowed and raw
Hollow out, as in a bark of pine,
A smile; and her mangy paw
Make for you a true cross's sign.

But it is her panting, shivering, bellowing sounds, her "music," her
"poetry" which is most significant, since of all the examples of suffering humanity described by Corbière, it is probably with her that
he most fervently identified himself. This raw, unpolished, discordant music which somehow merited transcendent stature may be
seen to presage the type of "music" which Tristan was to create
subsequently in order to expose (or to mask) his own private inferno:

Mais une note pantelante,
Écho grelottant dans le vent
Vient battre la rumeur bêlante
De ce purgatoire ambulant.
[ . . . ]
Elle hâle comme une plainte,

Comme une plainte de la faim,
Et, longue comme un jour sans pain,
Lamentablement, sa complainte . . .

But a panting sound,
An echo shivering in the wind
Breaks the bleating noise hovering around
This wandering mass of those who have sinned.
[ . . . ]
She heaves like a complaint,
Like a protest of not being fed,
And, long as a day without bread,
Lamentably, her lament . . .

Just before Corbière, Baudelaire had sung of the "underdog"; for the latter, the aged, the poor, and the blind, among others, possessed a certain mystical quality which served as a springboard for the poet's imagination.[5] On the contrary, Corbière looked upon these "creatures" not with the detached objectivity of the Poet, but rather with the compassion and understanding which his own physical and spiritual suffering could so naturally dispense.

Our view of the gallery of Breton inhabitants would not be complete without mention of the *matelot*, the sailor, who represented the majority of all Bretons. The *gens de mer* reflect a Breton world which was fundamentally masculine, a sea-faring universe in which virility, valor, realism, and direct confrontation were sacred qualities. In fact, the sea was the "leading lady" for most sailors, and there was generally no place for women "on board."[6] The two maritime pieces which present us this aspect of Corbière's Brittany—the salty slang of the sea, the crass language, and the simple bravery of the *matelot*—are "Matelots" and "La Fin."

The simplicity of the sailors in "Matelots" is conveyed by their feeling that they are just sailors—nothing more, nothing less. And there is a simple pride of their trade which accompanies this self-perception:

—Eux ils sont matelots.—À travers les tortures,
Les luttes, les dangers, les larges aventures,
Leur *face-à-coups-de-hache* a pris un tic nerveux
D'insoucient dédain pour ce qui n'est pas Eux . . .

> —*They* are sailors.—Through tortures,
> Struggles, dangers, grand adventures,
> Their *hatchet-hewn-faces* have assumed a nervous display
> Of jaunty disdain for those who are not They . . .

The "hatchet-hewn-faces" recall, of course, the visage of Sainte-Anne; and the scorn they feel is directed toward the *terriens*, the "landlubbers." Both the unattractive physical features and simplicity of character are developed in subsequent stanzas and echo similar qualities already seen elsewhere in the portrayal of other Bretons:

> Cassés, défigurés, dépaysés, perclus:
> —Un œil en moins.—Et vous, en avez-vous en plus?
> —La fièvre-jaune.—Eh bien, et vous, l'avez-vous rose?
> —Une balafre.—Ah c'est signé! . . .C'est quelque chose!
> —Et le bras en pantenne.—Oui, c'est un biscaïen,
> Le reste c'est le bel ouvrage au chirurgien.
> [ . . . ]
> —Héros?—ils riraient bien! . . .—Non merci: matelots!
>
> Broken, disfigured, homesick, crippled from seafare:
> —Missing an eye.—And you, have you one to spare?
> —Yellow-fever.—Well, and you, is yours pink?
> —A scar.—Ah, it's signed! . . .Not bad, don't you think?
> —And a gimpy arm.—Yes, it's a musket, big as life,
> The rest is the work of a surgeon's knife.
> [ . . . ]
> —Heroes?—they'd really laugh! . . .—No thanks: sailors!

Above all, these sailors are "living poets," a "poème vivant," and their song, like the *rapsode*'s, and like Tristan's own verse, is untainted by polish or sophistication. The poem ends with a stanza which will serve us well as a transition to our discussion of both "La Fin" and *Rondels pour après*:

> Tel qu'une vieille coque, au sec et dégréée,
> Où vient encor parfois clapoter la marée:
> Âme-de-mer en peine est le vieux matelot
> Attendant, échoué . . .—quoi: la mort?
>                                              —Non, le flot.

> Like an old hull, dry-docked and unrigged, where the tide
> Comes now and then to splash by its side:
> A lost sea-soul, the old sailor is he
> Awaiting, aground . . .—what: death?
>
> —No, the sea.

Of all experiences, death is the most natural, the one to which the sailor is most accustomed. This must have been very close to Tristan, whose life was constantly threatened by its own end, and whose existence must have often seemed destined for no other "end" than to see its conclusion.[7] And it is death which, perhaps significantly, "terminates" *Les Amours jaunes*, in "La Fin" and the six lovely pieces of *Rondels pour après*.

"La Fin" is basically a parodic reply to Victor Hugo's "Oceano Nox." Despite the poses employed in his poetry, Corbière despised one in particular—that which was purely literary, i.e., which falsely represented a given reality, especially by traditional, artificial devices such as hyperbole and periphrasis. This phenomenon of the literary transmutation of reality is what is under attack in "La Fin."

Tristan demonstrates his resentment of Hugo's vicarious intimacy with the sea and the tragic end of sailors in a three-pronged attack, by substituting his own brand of harsh poignancy for the latter's elegiac lamentation and lyrical niceties; a conception of death as a natural, lived experience for its absurd literary apotheosis; and colloquial locutions for rhetorical expression. First, Corbière criticizes Hugo's stance as philosopher-poet who replaces feeling itself with commentary, reading "Oceano Nox" as a kind of rhetorical sermon in which Hugo defends the cosmic tragedy of the deceased sailors, while denying them the "beautés farouches du métier d'homme" ("ferocious beauties of the manly trade"),[8] that is, eliminating all their intrinsic "sailor-ness" in favor of a certain pity as well as an awe before the presence of death itself. Second, Corbière sees Hugo's perspective as that of a *terrien* who does not really comprehend the relationship between the sailors and death. Whereas Hugo creates a hierarchical relationship in which death is the dominant (dominating) protagonist, Corbière sees this type of poetic mourning as profanation. His title, "La Fin," is ironic in that he considers death not as an enemy or even the "end" of life, but as a natural part of the sailors' daily struggle, their profession, their very life, which, when it comes, represents a supreme liberation. Recalling the conclusion of "Matelots," the fourth stanza substitutes the sea (a way of life) for death (the end of same):

> —Sombrer—Sonder ce mot. Votre *mort* est bien pâle
> Et pas grand'chose à bord, sous la lourde rafale . . .
> Pas grand'chose devant le grand sourire amer
> Du matelot qui lutte.—Allons donc, de la place!—
> Vieux fantôme éventé, la Mort change de face:
> La Mer! . . .

> —Sink—Sound that word. Your *death* is quite pale
> And not much on board, in the heavy gale . . .
> Not much compared to the great bitter smile, you see,
> Of the struggling sailor.—Come on, clear a place!—
> Old bloated phantom, Death changes its face:
> The Sea! . . .

Finally, the tone and poetic vocabulary of "La Fin" are purposely antithetical to those of "Oceano Nox." To Hugo's sentimentality and pathos, Corbière opposes a crude maritime speech and a tone which is both chiding (toward Hugo) and sympathetically defensive (of the sailors). And whereas Hugo hyperbolizes death with what Corbière's father Édouard would call "analogies parfumées" ("perfumed analogies")—expressions such as "l'aveugle océan" ("the blind ocean"), "les sombres étendues" ("the somber expanses"), and "de lugubres histoires" ("mournful stories")—Corbière, conversely, equates death with life by investing his text with vitality in expressions such as "le grand sourire amer" ("the great bitter smile"), "le ventre amoureux / D'une fille de joie en rut, à moitié soûle" ("the amorous belly / Of a prostitute in heat, half drunk," to which he compares the ocean's swell), and "L'âme d'un matelot( . . . )Respire à chaque flot" ("A sailor's soul[ . . . ]Breathes at each wave").

## IV   "For After . . ."

There is no doubt that death is one of the obsessive themes which appear throughout *Les Amours jaunes,* from "Épitaphe" and many other poems in the first four sections ("Un jeune qui s'en va," "Paria," "Le Poète contumace," "Laisser-courre," "Décourageux," etc.) to earlier texts like "Matelots" and "La Fin." Whether the tone is ironic or realistic, Corbière, like Baudelaire, must have been pondering the liberating possibilities of death as opposed to the confining limitations of mortal existence. Although we are likely to remember Corbière for his innovative verve and irony which mark the majority of his poems, we cannot neglect the fact that *Les Amours jaunes* ends with the section *Rondels pour après*, comprised of six *berceuses* ("lullabies") sung posthumously to a child, whom we must assume to be the extension (reversion) of Corbière himself.

And this brings up another problem, perhaps the most intriguing one of all. If *Les Amours jaunes* ends with these *rondels*, does this mean that they supersede all the trickery, posing, and word-games which preceded? Does his previous poetry (the *rondels* were the last poems he wrote) lead, then, inexorably, to a comment on or a solution of death as the sole liberating force for Tristan? One critic, Henri Thomas, even states that these poems are a logical (how strange to use this word in regard to Tristan!) sequel of "Litanie du sommeil."[9] All these questions are highly problematic: what is clear is that the *rondels* were written shortly before Tristan's death, so that this theme was not a surprising one with which to end the volume. More curious, however, is the nature of these poems: even more than the poems of *Armor* and *Gens de mer*, they are so unlike the Corbière we have been looking at—yet another surprise!—that we must marvel that the same man was capable of writing such verse.

This astonished reaction must be a far-reaching one, since these poems have been all but neglected by literary critics, being overshadowed by the more typical and stylistically interesting pieces of the first four sections. The *rondels* have none of the linguistic manipulation, personal torment, or provincial realism of their predecessors. They are filled with lovely rhythms, strange and powerful imagery, and delicate sonorities; their theme is the (posthumous) return to the world of childhood which is simple, marvelous, visionary, and, in the context of the other poems of the volume, totally unrecognizable. Their mysterious, illogical language is closer to that of the Rimbaud of *Illuminations*, and the opposition of a world of childlike innocence to that of bourgeois mediocrity recalls many of the lyrical songs of another contemporary, Charles Cros. The use of italics throughout also isolates these poems tonally from the rest of the volume. Finally, they represent perhaps the greatest enigma surrounding this enigmatic figure: written as the opening pieces to what would have become a discrete volume, *Mirlitons*, they reflect a new, lyrical, visionary style which, had death not interrupted its natural development, might have allowed Tristan to join Rimbaud and others as a recognized precursor of what we may loosely term "modernity" in the French lyric tradition. But we shall never know: perhaps, on the other hand, Tristan was again smiling as he wrote these poems, knowing that they *would* be an enigma for posterity (hence, the possible ambiguity of the posthumous *"pour après," "for after,"* of the section's title), abruptly interrupted by a premature demise.

In terms of form the *rondels* are also extraordinary for their sectional unity: except for the opening piece, "Sonnet posthume," they are all *rondels* which have been altered from the classical form perfected in the fifteenth century by Charles d'Orléans (thirteen verses, two rhymes, varying refrains); they are all in italics; they are directed to the *enfant*; they point to renewal in a wonderful posthumous world, relying on the future tense; and they contain the same type of novel imagery. One of the imperatives for future Corbière critics is a comprehensive study of this final section of *Les Amours jaunes;* for our purposes here, we must content ourselves with a brief examination of two of these poems in an attempt to gain access to this different, "other" Corbière.

The fourth *rondel,* "Mirliton" ("Doggerel Verse": there is still a hint of irony, or at least a will to confound), is, like the first three ("Sonnet posthume," "Rondel," "Do, l'enfant, do . . ."), a call to sleep made by the poet to his extension, the child:

> *Dors d'amour, méchant ferreur de cigales!*
> *Dans le chendent qui te couvrira*
> *La cigale aussi pour toi chantera,*
> *Joyeuse, avec ses petites cymbales.*
>
> *La rosée aura des pleurs matinales;*
> *Et le muguet blanc fait un joli drap . . .*
> *Dors d'amour, méchant ferreur de cigales.*
>
> *Pleureuses en troupeau passeront les refales . . .*
>
> *La Muse camarde ici posera,*
> *Sur ta bouche noire encore elle aura*
> *Ces rimes qui vont aux moelles des pâles . . .*
> *Dors d'amour, méchant ferreur de cigales.*
>
> *Sleep in love, naughty cicada-smith!*
> *In the scutch-grass as your cover*
> *For you too the cicada will sing like no other,*
> *With its little cymbals, in bliss.*

*Morning tears will have the mist;*
*And the white lilies make a lively slip . . .*
*Sleep in love, naughty cicada-smith.*

*The weeping flock of squalls will pass forthwith . . .*

*Here will come the Muse, your deathly Mother,*
*Upon your still-black mouth she'll discover*
*These rhymes which go to the pale ones' pith . . .*
*Sleep in love, naughty cicada-smith.*

Love, death, and a curious natural surrounding are all infused into the delicate atmosphere of this poem. Particularly interesting is the peaceful coexistence of antitheses, to be found only in the world of this posthumous idyll (again, we are tempted to draw comparisons with some of the scenes in Rimbaud's *Illuminations*): tears and joy, the Muse of Death, death and rebirth, animals personified, the child and inanimate Nature. The "Dors" of the refrain is mildly reminiscent of the same expression which appeared in an early poem already discussed, "Au vieux Roscoff." What surprises and touches us most, however, is the strange imagery. The child is a *"méchant ferreur de cigales"* (he is elsewhere referred to as a *"décrocheur d'étoiles,"* "unhooker of stars"; a *"Chevaucheur de rayons,"* "Rider of rays"; a *"Museleur de voilette,"* "Muzzler of veils"; a *"voleur d'étincelles,"* "thief of sparks"; and a *"peigneur de comètes,"* "comber of comets"). He is endowed with marvelous talents, impossible in real life (and thus possible for Corbière, through this infantile intermediary, in his poetry, at least in *this* poetry). The expression comes from a sixteenth-century phrase, *ferrer les cigales,* "to work at vain tasks"; but in this world, nothing is vain, and the shoeing of cicadas (as if they were horses)—perhaps in his childlike visions or poetry, as suggested in vv. 9–11—is as likely as the cicadas' playing of cymbals, which follows in v. 4. The cicadas are not the only entities personified by Corbière's verse: we also witness the weeping dew (v. 5), the housekeeping lilies (v. 6), and the gusts of wind which weep as well (v. 8). Like Rimbaud's *Illuminations,* "understanding" the text is not what counts; rather, we should pay attention to the novelty of Corbière's poetic expression, his marvelous images, and the way he transforms the mortality of one so young (*"La Muse camarde,"* "ta bouche noire") into a vision of tranquil fantasy.

In the poem which follows, "Petit mort pour rire" (another gently ironic title, playing on another expression, *petit mot pour rire*, "a little joke": here, death is a "slight" event, to be regarded without the usual solemnity), the phenomenon of death, especially tragic (normally) for one so young, is again transformed into an experience of liberation:

> *Va vite, léger peigneur de comètes!*
> *Les herbes au vent seront tes cheveux;*
> *De ton œil béant jailliront les feux*
> *Follets, prisonniers dans les pauvres têtes . . .*
>
> *Les fleurs de tombeau qu'on nomme Amourettes*
> *Foisonneront plein ton rire terreux . . .*
> *Et les myosotis, ces fleurs d'oubliettes . . .*
>
> *Ne fais pas le lourd: cercueils de poètes*
> *Pour les croque-morts sont de simples jeux,*
> *Boîtes à violon qui sonnent le creux . . .*
> *Ils te croiront mort—Les bourgeois sont bêtes—*
> *Va vite, léger peigneur de comètes!*
>
> *Light comber of comets, speed by!*
> *The grass in the wind will be your hair;*
> *From your hollow eye will leap wisp-flairs,*
> *Which in wretched heads in prisons die . . .*
>
> *The Amourettes on the tombs placed nigh*
> *And these prison-flowers, the forget-me-ne'er . . .*
> *Will make your earthy laugh multiply . . .*
>
> *Don't play the heavy: poets' coffins, why,*
> *They're simple games for the pallbearers,*
> *Fiddle-boxes with a hollow air . . .*
> *They'll think you dead—Another bourgeois lie—*
> *Light comber of comets, speed by!*

The metaphor "comber of comets" is not as strange as it might appear at first, since its base is etymological: "comet" comes from the Greek *komē*, "hair." (The same type of image is used, for instance, by Cros, who compares a woman with her hair floating behind to a "vagabond comet" in "Scherzo.") Once again, the child

is endowed with supernatural powers. Again, the natural sur-
roundings, if not personified here, at least participate in the child's
portrayal: grass becomes his hair, fires dance out of his sockets, and
flowers people his laugh. If this world is strange, it is also misun-
derstood by the bourgeois masses of the real world. The "fires"
which shoot out do not explicitly represent anything in particular,
but, in their movement, light, and heat, suggest genius, imagination, or intensity. But for the *"pauvres têtes,"* the ordinary heads of
mediocre people, they are "prisoners." This prison is subtly echoed
in the *"oubliettes"* of v. 7: besides "prison," the word evokes *ou-
blier,* "to forget," which is the English translation of *"myosotis,"*
"forget-me-nots." (The subtlety here is a far cry from the blatant
verbal juggling of many earlier poems.) For the bourgeois, death is
final, and the coffin is simply a hollow box in which to place the
man/fiddle who, in death, has ceased to play his tune. But they are
wrong, since death is only the beginning of a wonderful renewal, for
the child in these *rondels* and—who can be sure?—perhaps for
Corbière himself, who, although an atheist of sorts, may well have
believed—at the very end of his sorrowful existence—in some re-
demptive return to innocence, in a world after death in which what
was (with the possible exception of the creative act itself) total failure in his "real" life might be eternally reversed.

## CHAPTER 6

# Conclusion: Tristan WHO?

A ND so, as in all paradoxes, we come back, cyclically, to the same question posed at the beginning of this study. To the first part of this ambiguous question (i.e., "What was Tristan's true identity?"), we shall never be able to supply a satisfactory answer. But the poet with no identity still has something identifiable to leave with us, "for after": his poetry. And this supplies us with the key to the answer of the second (implied) part of the question (i.e., "What, as readers unfamiliar with his work, can we do to remedy his present anonymity?").

Partly owing to recent critical studies,[1] we are now much more familiar with the legacy which Corbière has left to posterity: innovative language, in the form of slang, neologism, and colloquial vocabulary, picked up by Pound, Eliot, and other "moderns"; diversity and unpredictability which challenges and defies the active mind of the reader; unreserved expression, immediacy, mystery, paradox, and irony which today are taken for granted in much contemporary verse. But the paradox here is that, despite all this, Corbière is still alone (perhaps in his idyllic [after-] world of innocence?) and still a relative unknown. Even more ironic is the probability that, although rejected in his own time by a rather conservative and antagonistic milieu, Tristan, were he living today, would have stood a good chance of being regarded as a folk-hero by today's society which—"liberated" and receptive to change—has accepted, with open arms, "daring" mavericks like Elvis Presley, the Beatles, Bob Dylan, Andy Warhol, and Mel Brooks.

Although it is a commonplace that the "trick" of life is not how to accept good fortune, but how to turn adversity into achievement, we may note in concluding this study that this is precisely what Corbière's sole accomplishment was. Despite a painfully obvious failure in life—perhaps more poignant, because of his total isolation, than the failures of other *maudits* like Baudelaire, Rimbaud, Verlaine, and Mallarmé—he did leave us with one of the most extraordinary and puzzling volumes of poetry ever written. It is, moreover, indeed unfortunate that Corbière was not able to enjoy this "success," although we are tempted to think that there remained within the poet sufficient ego to appreciate the truly startling quality of his verse and to anticipate that perhaps one day it would earn him the audience, the respect, even the love he so desperately yearned for during his lifetime. If he lived in his father's literary shadow, it is also ironic that he would never know to what degree he had surpassed the one writer whom, in his early years, he so fervently desired to emulate. These "sentimental" elements, coupled with the sheer verse of his poetry, should be incentive enough for us to read, and struggle with, Corbière's verse and at least to recognize his name for what it did to change the face of poetry forever.

# Notes and References

### Chapter One

1. For more detailed biographical information, see Albert Sonnenfeld, *L'Œuvre poétique de Tristan Corbière,* pp. 9–46.

2. Perhaps better known for their son, Pol Kalig (a pseudonym), who made it possible (via Léo Trézenik) for Verlaine to read *Les Amours jaunes.*

3. As so often happens, there are various (theoretical) versions of this anecdote (see, e.g., Sonnenfeld, *L'Œuvre poétique de Tristan Corbière,* p. 35). According to Jean Rousselot, *Tristan Corbière,* p. 70, it was not to Aunt Léonie, but to a prostitute, that the heart was presented.

4. For biographical sketches, see *Charles Cros, Tristan Corbière: Œuvres complètes,* "Bibliothèque de la Pléiade," pp. 665–66. The title will be abbreviated to *OC* in subsequent references to this edition.

### Chapter Two

1. The term was coined by Verlaine, whose essays on Corbière, Rimbaud, and Mallarmé in August 1883 (republished by Léon Vanier the following year, and expanded in 1888 to include Marceline Desbordes-Valmore, Villiers de l'Isle-Adam, and "Pauvre Lélian," an anagram for Verlaine himself) defined the *maudits* in typically vague, and not very useful, terms: "Absolute by their imagination, absolute in their expression, absolute as the absolute monarchs of the best of centuries."

2. See also Rimbaud's "Ce qu'on dit au poète à propos de fleurs," directed against de Lisle's aestheticism.

3. Louis Forestier, "Charles Cros cent ans après," pp. 5–6.

4. Rémy de Gourmont, *Le Livre des Masques,* pp. 157–58.

5. Francis F. Burch, *Tristan Corbière, l'originalité des "Amours jaunes,"* p. 164.

6. The two most comprehensive studies of Corbière's lexical idiosyncrasies occur in chapter 2 of Christian Angelet, *La poétique de Tristan Corbière,* and chapter 5 of Michel Dansel, *Langage et modernité chez Tristan Corbière.*

7. Burch, p. 204.

8. For a thorough discussion of orthographical aberrations, see Dansel, pp. 33–44.

9. Dansel, p. 160.

## Chapter Three

1. For an examination of Corbière's use of lexical and semantic incongruity, see Angelet, pp. 49–63.

2. Sonnenfeld, *L'Œuvre poétique de Tristan Corbière*, p. 57.

3. Ida Levi, *Tristan Corbière, a Biographical and Critical Study,* p. 186.

4. Jules Laforgue, *Œuvres complètes*, V, ed. G. Jean-Aubry (Paris: Mercure de France, 1922–25), pp. 136–37.

5. *OC*, p. 683.

6. "Wanting to Die," from "The Butterfly Ought to Sing" in *The Art of Sylvia Plath: a Symposium,* ed. Charles Newman (Bloomington: Indiana University Press, 1970), p. 176.

7. Germain Delpuech, *Tristan Corbière, poète maudit*, p. 24.

8. For two fascinating studies of similar phenomena in seventeenth-century verse, see John C. Lapp, *The Esthetics of Negligence: La Fontaine's "Contes"*(Cambridge: Cambridge University Press, 1971), and Edwin M. Duval, "The Poet on Poetry in Théophile de Viau's *Élégie à une dame*," *MLN*, 90, May 1975.

9. In his index, p. 143, Angelet incorrectly uses the indefinite article. Burch, p. 89, is in agreement concerning this error: "Le Dantec is right, I think, in restoring the numeral 'I' of the original edition. . . . Several editions have substituted the article 'Un' for it." Rousselot (p. 78) even omits the article!

10. See Charles Pornon, *Anthologie (apocryphe) de la poésie française* (Paris: Nouvel Office d'Édition, 1963), pp. 78–80; and Paul Reboux and Charles Müller, *A la manière de* . . . (Paris: Grasset, 1963), p. 127.

11. See *Album Zutique*, ed. Pascal Pia (Paris: J.–J. Pauvert, 1962), especially the dizains of Cros (pp. 51, 167), Verlaine (pp. 137, 177, 201, 219), Valade (pp. 41, 97, 105, 125, 141, 193), and Ponchon (p. 181).

12. In his discussion of the ellipsis of articles, p. 46, Dansel, perhaps significantly, neglects the examples which occur in "I Sonnet."

13. Dansel, p. 158. P.-O. Walzer, in his introduction to the book (p. 13), does not agree with this judgment.

## Chapter Four

1. Albert Camus, *Le Mythe de Sisyphe* (Paris: Gallimard, 1942). The two passages to be cited appear on pp. 130 and 18–19, respectively.

2. The most detailed examination of this poem (although its orientation is thematic rather than textual) can be found in Keith H. Macfarlane, *Tristan Corbière dans "Les Amours jaunes,"* pp. 59–73.

3. Marshall Lindsay, *Le Temps jaune: Essais sur Corbière*, p. 17.

4. See Jean Starobinski, *L'Œil vivant* (Paris: Gallimard, 1961), pp. 191–240, for an absorbing discussion of a similar phenomenon in regard to Stendhal.

5. Henri Thomas, *Tristan le Dépossédé*, p. 108.

6. Macfarlane, pp. 186–210.

7. Macfarlane, p. 203.

8. For three excellent discussions of this problem, see Sonnenfeld, *L'Œuvre poétique de Tristan Corbière*, pp. 78–90; Macfarlane, pp. 78–125; and Thomas, pp. 27–61.

9. For references to the possible sources of the title of the volume, see Sonnenfeld, *L'Œuvre poétique de Tristan Corbière*, pp. 47–52; *OC*, p. 700; and Marshall Lindsay, "A Source of the Title *Les Amours jaunes:* La Landelle."

10. See Corbière's poem "Steam-Boat."

11. How different, also, from the sexual problems (and proposed solutions) of the adolescent Rimbaud, who planned to "reinvent love"! For an illuminating analysis of the latter, see Enid Rhodes Peschel, *Flux and Reflux: Ambivalence in the Poems of Arthur Rimbaud* (Geneva: Droz, 1977), pp. 87–102.

12. Jules Laforgue, "Une Étude sur Tristan Corbière, " p. 4.

13. Macfarlane, p. 125.

## Chapter Five

1. For example, P.-O. Walzer, in *OC*, p. 685.

2. Sonnenfeld, *L'Œuvre poétique de Tristan Corbière*, p. 120.

3. Sonnenfeld, "Tristan Corbière: the Beatific Malediction," p. 40.

4. For a brief discussion of La Landelle's influence, see *OC*, p. 673.

5. This attitude is apparent in poems like "Les Sept vieillards," "Les Petites vieilles," and "Les Aveugles"; and in the prose poem "Les Fenêtres."

6. See, for example, Corbière's prose piece, *L'Américaine*.

7. The most detailed discussion of this theme is in Macfarlane, pp. 126–82.

8. The expression is used by André Rousseaux in "Situation de Tristan Corbière."

9. In his preface to the 1973 Gallimard edition of *Les Amours jaunes*, p. 11.

## Chapter Six

1. Any meaningful discussion of this complex problem would require a separate volume, falling outside of the scope of this one. For an introduction to Corbière's influence on "modern" poets, however, see Sonnenfeld, *L'Œuvre poétique de Tristan Corbière*, pp. 176–97; Burch, pp. 185–215; and Dansel, pp. 141–64.

# Selected Bibliography

PRIMARY SOURCES

*Les Amours jaunes*. Paris: Librairie du XIXe siecle, Glady frères, 1873.
*Les Amours jaunes*, ed. Alexandre Arnoux. Paris: Librarie Celtique, 1947.
*Les Amours jaunes*, ed. Tristan Tzara. Paris: Le Club français du Livre, 1950.
*Les Amours jaunes*, ed. Yves-Gérard Le Dantec. Paris: Gallimard, 1953.
*Charles Cros, Tristan Corbière: Œuvres complètes*, ed. P.-O. Walzer. Paris: Bibliothèque de la Pléiade, Gallimard, 1970.
*Les Amours jaunes*, ed. Jean-Louis Lalanne. Preface by Henri Thomas. Paris: Poésie, Gallimard, 1973.
*Catalogue d'exposition. Tristan Corbière: 1845-1875*. Morlaix: Musée de Morlaix, 1975.

SECONDARY SOURCES

The following is a list of all books entirely devoted to Corbière, as well as other publications which I consider to be of particular interest (books partially devoted to Corbière, articles, correspondence). Since the dearth of biographical information has tended to invite critical studies which are hypothetical or even arbitrary, I have omitted many shorter studies which seem to me to be of dubious value. Because the publications of the second group mentioned above are, in many cases, limited in their contribution to our understanding of the poetry itself, I have included thumbnail evaluations only for books devoted solely to Corbière.

ANGELET, CHRISTIAN. *La Poétique de Tristan Corbière*. Brussels: Palais des Académies, 1961. The first thorough inventory of Corbière's stylistic innovations. Indispensable.
ARNOUX, ALEXANDRE. *Une âme et pas de violon . . .Tristan Corbière*. Paris: Grasset, 1929. An ultrastylized recounting of Corbière's life: as biography, interesting but generally unreliable.
BLÉMONT, ÉMILE. "Les Amours jaunes." *La Renaissance artistique et littéraire*, 2, 26 October 1873.
BLOY, LÉON. "On demande des malédictions." *Le Chat Noir*, 3 May 1884.

BOCQUET, LÉON. *Les Destinées mauvaises*. Amiens: E. Malfère, 1923.

BRETON, ANDRÉ. *Anthologie de l'humour noir*. Paris: J.-J. Pauvert, 1966.

BURCH, FRANCIS F. *Tristan Corbière, l'originalité des "Amours jaunes" et leur influence sur T. S. Eliot*. Paris: Nizet, 1970. Extremely useful study of literary development of Corbière; particularly interesting are concluding discussions of the linguistic and thematic affinities between the two poets.

———. *Sur Tristan Corbière*. Paris: Nizet, 1975. Annotated collection of the first critical studies of Corbière (1873–1912) and letters to, and about, the poet. Valuable for its presentation of previously inaccessible material.

DANSEL, MICHEL. *Langage et modernité chez Tristan Corbière*. Paris: Nizet, 1974. A poet's perceptions of a poet. Similar to Angelet's stylistic study, with more of an accent on the significance of Corbière's innovation for posterity. Also indispensable.

DELPUECH, GERMAIN. *Tristan Corbière, poète maudit*. Paris: Charles-Lavauzelle, 1966. A speech which gives a bird's-eye view of Tristan's life and work. Uninspiring.

GESLIN, OLIVIER. *L'Œuvre poétique et la vie de Tristan Corbière*. Saint-Brieuc: Presses bretonnes, 1975. A slight pamphlet of dubious value which says nothing new, despite its pretentious title.

GOURMONT, RÉMY DE. *Le Livre des Masques*. 17th ed. Paris: Mercure de France, 1923.

GRIN, MICHA. *Tristan Corbière, poète maudit*. Évian: Éd. du Nant d'Enfer, 1972. Useless bibliography, material borrowed from books not cited, pretentious.

HUYSMANS, JORIS-KARL. *À rebours*. Paris: Charpentier, 1884.

LAFORGUE, JULES. "Notes sur Baudelaire, Corbière, Mallarmé, Rimbaud." *Entretiens politiques et littéraires*, 2, April, July 1891.

———. *Œuvres complètes*, V, ed. G. Jean-Aubry. Paris: Mercure de France, 1922–25, pp. 136–37.

LEVI, IDA. "New Light on Tristan Corbière." *French Studies*, 5, July 1951.

———. *Tristan Corbière, a Biographical and Critical Study*. Diss. Oxford, 1951. Some interesting hypotheses, not much on poetry.

LINDSAY, MARSHALL. *Le Temps jaune: Essais sur Corbière*. Berkeley: University of California Press, 1972. Uneven and often misleading, but intelligent and with some fine insights on Corbière's poetic strategy.

———. "A Source of the Title *Les Amours jaunes*: La Landelle." *Modern Language Notes*, 75, December 1960.

———. "The Versification of Corbière's *Les Amours jaunes*." *PMLA*, 78, September 1963.

MACFARLANE, KEITH H. *Tristan Corbière dans "Les Amours jaunes."* Paris: Minard, 1974. The most comprehensive study of Corbière's poetry and internal drama to date. Absolutely first-rate and indispensable.

MARTINEAU, RENÉ. *Tristan Corbière*. Paris: Le Divan, 1925. The first thorough biography, but often limited by hypothesis.

MITCHELL, ROBERT L. "The Muted Fiddle: Tristan Corbière's 'I Sonnet' as *Ars (Im)poetica*." *French Review*, 50, October 1976.

———. "Corbière, Hélas!: A Case of *Antirayonnement*." *French Review*, 51, February 1978.

———. "Malédiction et résurrection: L'Accueil critique de Tristan Corbière depuis 1960." *Œuvres et Critiques*, 4, No. 2 (1979).

NEWMAN-GORDON, PAULINE. *Corbière-Laforgue-Apollinaire ou le rire en pleurs*. Paris: Nouvelles Éditions Debresse, 1964.

NOULET, ÉMILIE. *Le Ton poétique*. Paris: José Corti, 1971.

QUENNELL, PETER. *Baudelaire and the Symbolists*. 2nd ed. London: Weidenfeld and Nicolson, 1954.

ROUSSEAUX, ANDRÉ. "Situation de Tristan Corbière." *Le Figaro littéraire*, 13 March 1954.

ROUSSELOT, JEAN. *Tristan Corbière*. Paris: Poètes d'aujourd'hui, Seghers, 1951. A generalized but compact and useful guide to the essential themes in Corbière's poetry. Followed by a representative choice of texts.

SCHNEIDER, PIERRE. *La Voix vive*. Paris: Éditions de Minuit, 1953.

SONNENFELD, ALBERT. *L'Œuvre poétique de Tristan Corbière*. Paris: Presses Universitaires de France/Princeton University Press, 1960. The first important book on Corbière. A comprehensive study of biography, thematics, and influence, it is the reference point of much Corbière criticism written since. Indispensable.

———. "The Yellow Laugh of Corbière." *Yale French Studies*, 23, summer 1959.

———. "Tristan Corbière: The Beatific Malediction." *L'Esprit créateur*, 9, spring 1969.

STEPHAN, PHILIP. "Problems of Structure in the Poetry of Tristan Corbière." *Modern Language Quarterly*, 22, December 1961.

THOMAS, HENRI. *Tristan le Dépossédé*. Paris: Gallimard, 1972. Like Dansel's book, a poet's view of a poet. A perhaps-too-logical but fascinating account of Corbière's journey toward "self-exorcism." Some extremely valuable insights.

TRÉZENIK, LÉO. "Notes sur Corbière." *La Plume*, 15 August 1891.

TZARA, TRISTAN. "Tristan Corbière ou les limites du cri." *Europe*, 28, December 1950.

VERLAINE, PAUL. *Les Poètes maudits*. Paris: Vanier, 1884.

WALZER, P.-O. *La Révolution des Sept*. Neuchâtel: La Baconnière, 1970.

———. "Autour du centenaire de Tristan Corbière." *RHLF*, 76, March-April 1976.

# Index